General contents

Europe and the global information society

Recommendations of the high-level group
on the information society to the Corfu European Council
(Bangemann group)

In its Brussels meeting of December 1993, the European Council requested that a report be prepared for its meeting on 24 and 25 June 1994 in Corfu by a group of prominent persons on the specific measures to be taken into consideration by the Community and the Member States for the infrastructures in the sphere of information. On the basis of this report, the Council will adopt an operational programme defining precise procedures for action and the necessary means.

The following were members of the group chaired by Mr Martin Bangemann, Member of the Commission:

Peter L. Bonfield (Chairman and Chief Executive, ICL), Enrico Cabral da Fonseca (Presidente Companhia Comunicaçaoes nacionais), Etienne Davignon (Président, SGB), Peter J. Davis (Chairman, Reed Elsevier), Jean-Marie Descarpentries (Président Bull), Carlo De Benedetti (Presidente Amministratore Delegato, Olivetti), Brian Ennis (Managing Director, IMS), Pehr G. Gyllenhammer (former Executive Chairman, AB Volvo), Hans Olaf Henkel (Chairman and Chief Executive Officer, IBM Europe), Anders Knutsen (Administrerende Direktor, Bang & Olufsen), Pierre Lescure (Président Directeur, Général Canal +), Constantin Makropoulos (former Managing Director, ELSYP (Hellenic Information Systems)), Pascual Maragall (Alcalde de Barcelona, Vicepresidente de POLIS), Lothar Hunsel (designierter Vorsitzender der Geschäftsführung DeTeMobilfunk GmbH), Romano Prodi (Presidente Direttore Generale, IRI), Gaston Egmont Thorn (Président du Conseil d'administration du CLT), Jan D. Timmer (Voorzitter, Philips Electronics), Cándido Velázquez Gastelu (Presidente, Telefónica), Heinrich von Pierer (Vorsitzender des Vorstandes, Siemens AG).

Contents

This report urges the European Union to put its faith in market mechanisms as the motive power to carry us into the information age.

This means that actions must be taken at the European level and by Member States to strike down entrenched positions which put Europe at a competitive disadvantage:

☐ it means fostering an entrepreneurial mentality to enable the emergence of new dynamic sectors of the economy

☐ it means developing a common regulatory approach to bring forth a competitive, Europe-wide, market for information services

☐ it does NOT mean more public money, financial assistance, subsidies, *dirigisme,* or protectionism.

In addition ot its specific recommendations, the group proposes an action plan of concrete initiatives based on a partnership between the private and public sectors to carry Europe forward into the information society.

Chapter 1: The information society — new ways of living and working together

A revolutionary challenge to decision makers

Throughout the world, information and communication technologies are generating a new industrial revolution already as significant and far-reaching as those of the past.

It is a revolution based on information, itself the expression of human knowledge. Technological progress now enables us to process, store, retrieve and communicate information in whatever form it may take, whether oral, written or visual, unconstrained by distance, time and volume.

This revolution adds huge new capacities to human intelligence and constitutes a resource which *changes the way we both work and live together.*

Europe is already participating in this revolution, but with an approach which is still too fragmentary and which could reduce expected benefits. An information society is a means to achieve so many of the Union's objectives. We have to get it right, and get it right now.

Partnership for jobs

Europe's ability to participate, to adapt and to exploit the new technologies and the opportunities they create, will require partnership between individuals, employers, unions and governments dedicated to managing change. If we manage the changes before us with determination and understanding of the social implications, we shall all gain in the long run.

Our work has been sustained by the conviction expressed in the Commission's White Paper, 'Growth, Competitiveness and Employment', that '...the enormous potential for new services relating to production, consumption, culture and leisure activities will create large numbers of new jobs...'. Yet nothing will happen automatically. We have to act to ensure that these jobs are created here, and soon. And that means public and private sectors acting together.

If we seize the opportunity

All revolutions generate uncertainty, discontinuity and opportunity. Today's is no exception. How we respond and how we turn current opportunities into real benefits, will depend on how quickly we can enter the European information society.

In the face of quite remarkable technological developments and economic opportunities, all the leading global industrial players are reassessing their strategies and their options.

A common creation or a still fragmented Europe?

The first countries to enter the information society will reap the greatest rewards. They will set the agenda for all who must follow. By contrast, countries which temporize, or favour half-hearted solutions, could, in less than a decade, face disastrous declines in investment and a squeeze on jobs.

Given its history, we can be sure that Europe will take the opportunity. It will create the information society. *The only question is whether this will be a strategic creation for the whole Union, or a more fragmented and much less effective* *amalgam of individual initiatives by Member States,* with repercussions on every policy area, from the single market to cohesion.

What we can expect for . . .

☐ Europe's citizens and consumers:
A more caring European society with a significantly higher quality of life and a wider choice of services and entertainment.

☐ The content creators:
New ways to exercise their creativity as the information society welcomes new products and services.

☐ Europe's regions:
New opportunities to express their cultural traditions and identities and, for those standing on the geographical periphery of the Union, a minimizing of distance and remoteness.

☐ Governments and administrations:
More efficient, transparent and responsive public services, closer to the citizen and at lower cost.

☐ European business and small and medium-sized enterprises:
More effective management and organization, access to training and other services, data links with customers and suppliers generating greater competitiveness.

☐ Europe's telecommunications operators:
The capacity to supply an ever wider range of new high value-added services.

☐ The equipment and software suppliers; the computer and consumer electronics industries.
New and strongly-growing markets for their products at home and abroad.

The social challenge

The widespread availability of new information tools and services will present fresh opportunities to build a more equal and balanced society and to foster individual accomplishment. *The information society has the potential to improve the quality of life of Europe's citizens, the efficiency of our social and economic organization and to reinforce cohesion.*

The information revolution prompts profound changes in the way we view our societies and also in their organization and structure. This presents us with a major challenge: either we grasp the opportunities before us and master the

risks, or we bow to them, together with all the uncertainties this may entail.

The main risk lies in the creation of a two-tier society of have and have-nots, in which only a part of the population has access to the new technology, is comfortable using it and can fully enjoy its benefits. There is a danger that individuals will reject the new information culture and its instruments.

Such a risk is inherent in the process of structural change. We must confront it by convincing people that the new technologies hold out the prospect of a major step forward towards a European society less subject to such constraints as rigidity, inertia and compartmentalization. By pooling resources that have traditionally been separate, and indeed distant, the information infrastructure unleashes unlimited potential for acquiring knowledge, innovation and creativity.

Mastering risks, maximizing benefits

Thus, we have to find ways to master the risks and maximize the benefits. This places responsibilities on public authorities to establish safeguards and to ensure the cohesion of the new society. Fair access to the infrastructure will have to be guaranteed to all, as will provision of universal service, the definition of which must evolve in line with the technology.

A great deal of effort must be put into securing widespread public acceptance and actual use of the new technology. *Preparing Europeans for the advent of the information society is a priority task. Education, training and promotion will necessarily play a central role.* The White Paper's goal of giving European citizens the right to life-long education and training here

finds its full justification. In order best to raise awareness, regional and local initiatives, whether public or private should be encouraged.

The arrival of the information society comes in tandem with changes in labour legislation and the rise of new professions and skills. Continuous dialogue between the social partners will be extremely important if we are to anticipate and to manage the imminent transformation of the workplace. This concerted effort should reflect new relationships at the workplace induced by the changing environment.

More detailed consideration of these issues exceeds the scope of this report. The group wishes to stress that Europe is bound to change, and that it is in our interest to seize this opportunity. The information infrastructure can prove an extraordinary instrument for serving the people of Europe and improving our society by fully reflecting the original and often unique values which underpin and give meaning to our lives.

At the end of the day, the added value brought by the new tools, and the overall success of the information society, will depend on the input made by our people, both individually and in working together. We are convinced that Europeans will meet this challenge.

Time to press on

Why the urgency? Because competitive suppliers of networks and services from outside Europe are increasingly active in our markets. They are convinced, as we must be, that if Europe arrives late our suppliers of technologies and services will lack the commercial muscle to win a share of the enormous global opportunities which lie ahead. Our companies will migrate to more attractive locations to do business. Our export markets will evaporate. We have to prove them wrong.

Tide waits for no man, and this is a revolutionary tide, sweeping through economic and social life. We must press on. At least we do not have the usual European worry about catching up. In some areas we are well placed, in others we do

need to do more. However this is also true for the rest of the world's trading nations.

The importance of the sector was made evident by its prominence during the Uruguay Round of GATT negotiations. This importance is destined to increase.

We should not be sceptical of our possibilities for success. We have major technological, entrepreneurial and creative capabilities. However, the diffusion of information is still too restricted and too expensive. This can be tackled quickly through regulatory reforms.

Public awareness of the technologies has hitherto been too limited. This must change. *Political attention is too intermittent. The private sector expects a new signal.*

An action plan

This report outlines our vision of the information society and the benefits it will deliver to our citizens and to economic operators. It points to areas in which action is needed now so we can start out on the market-led passage to the new age, as well as to the agents which can drive us there.

As requested in the Council's mandate, we advocate an action plan based on specific initiatives involving partnerships linking public and private sectors. Their objective is to stimulate markets so that they can rapidly attain critical mass.

In this sector, private investment will be the driving force. Monopolistic, anticompetitive environments are the real roadblocks to such involvement. The situation here is completely different from that of other infrastructural investments where public funds are still crucial, such as transport.

This sector is in rapid evolution. *The market will drive,* it will decide on winners and losers. Given the power and pervasiveness of the technology, this market is global.

The prime task of government is to safeguard competitive forces and ensure a strong and lasting political welcome for the information society, so that demand-pull can finance growth, here as elsewhere.

By sharing our vision, and appreciating its urgency, Europe's decision-makers can make the prospects for our renewed economic and social development infinitely brighter.

New markets in Europe's information society

Information has a multiplier effect which will energize every economic sector. With market driven tariffs, there will be a vast array of novel information services and applications:

☐ from high-cost services, whose premium prices are justified by the value of benefits delivered, to budget price products designed for mass consumption;

☐ from services to the business community, which can be tailored to the needs of a specific customer, to standardized packages which will sell in high volumes at low prices;

☐ from services and applications which employ existing infrastructure, peripherals and equipment (telephone and cable TV networks, broadcasting systems, personal computers, CD players and ordinary TV sets) to those which will be carried via new technologies, such as integrated broadband, as these are installed.

Markets for business

Large and small companies and professional users are already leading the way in exploiting the new technologies to raise the efficiency of their management and production systems. And more radical changes to business organization and methods are on the way.

Business awareness of these trends and opportunities is still lower in Europe compared to the US. Companies are not yet fully exploiting the potential for internal reorganization and for adapting relationships with suppliers, contractors and customers. We have a lot of pent up demand to fill.

In the business markets, teleconferencing is one good example of a business application worth promoting, while much effort is also being dedicated worldwide to the perfection of telecommerce and electronic document interchange (EDI).

Both offer such cost and time advantages over traditional methods that, once applied, electronic procedures rapidly become the preferred way of doing business. According to some estimates the handling of an electronic requisition is one tenth of the cost of handling its paper equivalent, while an electronic mail (E-mail) message is faster, more reliable and can save 95% of the cost of a fax.

Electronic payments systems are already ushering in the cashless society in some parts of Europe. We have a sizeable lead over the rest of the world in smart-card technology and applications. This is an area of global market potential.

Markets for small and medium-sized enterprises

Though Europe's 12 million SMEs are rightly regarded as the backbone of the European economy, they do need to manage both information and managerial resources better.

They need to be linked to easy access, cost-effective networks providing information on production and market openings. The competitiveness of the whole industrial fabric would be sharpened if their relationships with large companies were based on the new technologies.

Networked relationships with universities, research institutes and laboratories would boost their prospects even more by helping to remedy chronic R&D deficiencies. Networking will also diminish the isolation of SMEs in Europe's less advantaged regions, helping them to upgrade their products and find wider markets.

Markets for consumers

These are expected to be richly populated with services, from home banking and teleshopping to a near-limitless choice of entertainment on demand.

In Europe, like the United States, mass consumer markets may emerge as one of the principal driving forces for the information society.

American experience already shows that the development markets encounter a number of obstacles and uncertainties.

Given the initial high cost of new pay-as-you-view entertainment services, and of the related equipment, as well as the high cost of bringing fibre optics to the home, a large mass consumer market will develop more easily if entertainment services are part of a broader package. This could also include information data, cultural programming, sporting events, as well as telemarketing and teleshopping. Pay-as-you-view for on-line services, as well as advertising, will both be necessary as a source of revenue. To some extent, existing satellite and telephone infrastructure can help to serve the consumer market in the initial phase.

At the moment, this market is still only embryonic in Europe and is likely to take longer to grow than in the United States. There, more than 60% of households are tapped by cable TV systems which could also carry text and data services. In Europe, only 25% are similarly equipped, and this figure masks great differences between countries, e.g. Belgium (92%) and Greece (1 to 2%).

Another statistic: in the United States there are 34 PCs per hundred citizens. The European figure overall is 10 per hundred, though the UK, for instance, at 22 per hundred, is closer to the US level of computer penetration.

Lack of available information services and poor computer awareness could therefore prove handicaps in Europe. Telecommunication networks are, however, comparable in size and cover, but lag behind in terms of utilization. These networks, therefore, can act as the basic port of access for the initial services, but stimulation of user applications is still going to be necessary.

Such structural weaknesses need not halt progress. Europe's technological success with CD-ROM and CD-I could be the basis for a raft of non-networked applications and services during the early formative years of the information society. These services on disk have considerable export potential if Europe's audio-visual industry succeeds in countering current US dominance in titles.

In terms of the market, France's *Minitel* network already offers an encouraging example that European consumers are prepared to buy information and transaction services on screen, if the access price is right. It reaches nearly 30 million private and business subscribers through six million small terminals and carries about 15 000 different services. Minitel has created many new jobs, directly and indirectly, through boosting business efficiency and competitiveness.

In the UK, the success of the Community-sponsored 'Homestead' programme, using CD-I, is indicative, as is the highly successful launch of a dedicated (American) cable teleshopping channel.

Meanwhile in the US, where the consumer market is more advanced, video-on-demand and home shopping could emerge as the most popular services.

Audio-visual markets

Our biggest structural problem is the financial and organizational weakness of the European programme industry. Despite the enormous richness of the European heritage, and the potential of our creators, most of the programmes and most of the stocks of acquired rights are not in European hands. A fast growing European home market can provide European industry with an opportunity to develop a home base and to exploit increased possibilities for exports.

Linguistic fragmentation of the market has long been seen as a disadvantage for Europe's entertainment and audio-visual industry, especially with English having an overwhelming dominance in the global market — a reflection of the US lead in production and, importantly, in distribution. This lead, which begins with cinema and continues with television, is likely to be extended to the new audio-visual areas. However, *once products can be easily accessible to consumers, there will be more opportunities for expression of the multiplicity of cultures and languages in which Europe abounds.*

Europe's audio-visual industry is also burdened with regulations. Some of these will soon be rendered obsolete by the development of new technologies, hampering the development of a dynamic European market.

As a first step to stimulating debate on the new challenges, the Commission has produced a Green Paper on the audiovisual industry.

Chapter 2: A market-driven revolution

A break with the past

The group is convinced that technological progress and the evolution of the market mean that Europe must make a break from policies based on principles which belong to a time before the advent of the information revolution.

The key issue for the emergence of new markets is the need for a new regulatory environment allowing full competition. This will be a prerequisite for mobilizing the private capital necessary for innovation, growth and development.

In order to function properly, the new market requires that all actors are equipped to participate successfully, or at least that they do not start with significant handicaps. All should be able to operate according to clear rules, within a single, fair and competitive framework.

> **The group recommends Member States to accelerate the ongoing process of liberalization of the telecom sector by:**
>
> - **opening up to competition infrastructures and services still in the monopoly area**
>
> - **removing non-commercial political burdens and budgetary constraints imposed on telecommunications operators**
>
> - **setting clear timetables and deadlines for the implementation of practical measures to achieve these goals**

Ending monopoly

This is as true for the telecommunications operators (TOs) as for others. It is now generally recognized as both necessary and desirable that the political burdens on them should be removed, their tariffs adjusted and a proper regulatory framework created. Even the operations of those TOs whose status has already evolved over recent years are not fully in line.

It is possible to end monopoly. In future, all licensed public operators should assume their share of public service responsibilities (e.g. universal service obligation and the provision of equal access to networks and services).

A competitive environment requires the following:

☐ TOs relieved of political constraints, such as:

subsidizing public functions;
external R&D activities;
contributions to land planning and management objectives;
the burden to carry alone the responsibility of universal service;

☐ a proper regulatory framework designed to achieve:

market regulation to enable and to protect competition;

a predictable environment to make possible strategic planning and investment;

☐ adjustment of tariffs.

Enabling the market

> **The group recommends the establishment at the European level of an authority whose terms of reference will require prompt attention.**

In order for the market to operate successfully, the group has identified the following objectives and recommendations:

Evolution in the regulatory domain

Identify and establish the minimum of regulation needed, at the European level, to ensure the rapid emergence of efficient European information infrastructures and services. The terms of reference of the authority which will be responsible for the enforcement of this regulation is a question that will require prompt attention.

The urgency of the matter is in direct relation to the prevailing market conditions. A clear requirement exists for the new 'rules of the game' to be outlined as soon as possible. The marketplace will then be in a position to anticipate the forthcoming framework, and the opportunity will exist for those wishing to move rapidly to benefit from these efforts.

The authority will need to address:

☐ the regulation of those operations which, because of their Community-wide nature, need to be addressed at European level, such as licensing, network interconnection when and where necessary, management of shared scarce resources (e.g. radio-frequency allocation, subscriber numbering) and advice to Member States' regulatory authorities on general issues.

☐ a single regulatory framework valid for all operators, which would imply lifting unequal conditions for market access. It would also ensure that the conditions for network access and

service use would be guided by the principles of transparency and non-discrimination, complemented by practical rules for dispute resolution and speedy remedy against abuse dominance.

Interconnection and interoperability

Two features are essential to the deployment of the information infrastructure needed by the information society: one is a seamless interconnection of networks and the other that the services and applications which build on them should be able to work together (interoperability).

In the past the political will to interconnect national telephone networks resulted in hundreds of millions of subscriber connections worldwide. Similar political determination and corresponding effort are required to set up the considerably more complex information infrastructures.

> **Interconnection of networks and interoperability of services and applications are recommended as primary Union objectives.**

The challenge is to provide interconnections for a variety of networking conditions (e.g. fixed and new type of networks, such as mobile and satellite) and basic services (e.g. integrated service digital network (ISDN)). Currently, the positions of monopoly operators are being eroded in these fast-developing areas.

Joint commercial decisions must be taken by the TOs without delay to ensure rapid extension of European basic services beyond telephony. This would improve their competitive position vis-à-vis non-European players in their own markets.

The European information society is emerging from many different angles. European infrastructure is evolving into an ever tighter web of networks, generic services, applications and equipment, the development, distribution and maintenance of which occupy a multitude of sources worldwide.

In an efficient and expanding information infrastructure, such components should work together.

Assembling the various pieces of this complex system to meet the challenge of interoperability would be impossible without clear conventions. 'Standards' are such conventions.

Open 'systems standards' will play an essential role in building a European information infrastructure.

Standards institutes have an honourable record in producing European standards, but the standardization process as it stands today raises a number of concerns about fitness for purpose, lack of interoperability, and priority setting that is not sufficiently market-driven.

Action is required at three different levels:

☐ **at the level of operators, public procurement and investors:**

Following the successful example of GSM digital mobile telephony, market players (industry, TOs, users) could establish memoranda of understanding (MoU) to set the specifications requirements for specific application objectives. These requirements would then provide input to the competent standardization body. This type of mechanism would adequately respond to market needs.

Operators, public procurement and investors should adopt unified open standard-based solutions for the provision and the procurement of information services in order to achieve global interoperability.

☐ **at the level of the European standards bodies:**

These should be encouraged to establish priorities based on market requirements and to identify publicly available specifications, originated by the market, which are suitable for rapid transformation into standards (e.g. through fast-track procedures).

☐ **at the level of the Union:**

European standardization policy should be reviewed in the light of the above. When the market is not providing acceptable technical solutions to achieve one of the European Union's objectives, a mechanism should be sought to select or generate suitable technologies.

World-wide interoperability should be promoted and secured.

> **The group recommends a review of the European standardization process in order to increase its speed and responsiveness to markets.**

Urgent action to adjust tariffs

Reduction in international, long distance and leased-line tariffs will trigger expansion in the usage of infrastructures, generating additional revenues, and simultaneously giving a major boost to generic services and innovative applications.

In most cases, the current unsatisfactory tariff situation results from the TOs' monopoly status and a variety of associated political constraints.

The introduction of competitive provision of services and infrastructures implies that TOs would be able to adjust their tariffs in line with market conditions. Rebalancing of international and long-distance tariffs against local tariffs is a critical step in this process.

> The group recommends as a matter of
> urgency the adjustment of international,
> long distance and leased line tariffs to
> bring these down into line with rates
> practised in other advanced industrial-
> ized regions. Adjustment of tariffs should
> be accompanied by the fair-sharing of
> public service obligations among opera-
> tors.

Two elements should accompany the process:

☐ TOs released from politically imposed budgetary constraints;

☐ a fair and equitable sharing of the burden of
providing universal services between all licensed
operators.

Fostering critical mass

Market segments based on the new information
infrastructures cannot provide an adequate return
on investment without a certain level of demand.
In most cases, competition alone will not provide such a mass, or it will provide it too slowly.

A number of measures should be taken in order
to reach this goal:

☐ cooperation should be encouraged among
competitors so as to create the required size and
momentum in particular market areas. The already mentioned GSM MoU is an archetypal
example of how positive this approach can be.

☐ agreement between public administrations to
achieve common requirements and specifications, and a commitment to use these in procurement at national and European levels.

☐ extensive promotion and use of existing and
forthcoming European networks and services.

☐ awareness campaigns, notably directed at
public administrations, SMEs and educational
institutions.

> It is recommended to promote public
> awareness. Particular attention should be
> paid to the small and medium-sized busi-
> ness sector, public administrations and
> the younger generation.

In addition, everyone involved in building up the
information society must be in a position to
adapt strategies and forge alliances to enable
them to contribute to, and benefit from, overall
growth in the field.

Secure the world-wide dimension

> The group recommends that the open-
> ness of the European market should find
> its counterpart in markets and networks
> of other regions of the world. It is of
> paramount importance for Europe that
> adequate steps are taken to guarantee
> equal access.

Since information infrastructures are borderless
in an open market environment, the information
society has an essentially global dimension.

The actions advocated in this report will lead to
a truly open environment, where access is provided to all players. This openness should find
its counterpart in markets and networks of other
regions of the world. It is obviously of paramount importance for Europe that adequate steps
are taken to guarantee equal access.

Towards a positive outcome

The responses outlined above to the challenges posed by the deployment of the information society will be positive for all involved in its creation and use.

Telecommunications, cable and satellite operators will be in a position to take full advantage of market opportunities as they see fit, and to expand their market share.

The service provider and content industries will be able to offer innovative products at attractive prices.

Citizens and users will benefit from a broader range of competing services.

Telecommunication equipment and software suppliers will see an expanding market.

Those countries that have already opted for faster liberalization, are experiencing rapidly expanding domestic markets that provide new opportunities for TOs, service providers and industry. For the others, the price to pay for a slower pace of liberalization will be a stiffer challenge from more dynamic foreign competitors and a smaller domestic market. Time is running out. If action is not accelerated, many benefits will arrive late, or never.

It is an essential recommendation of the group that governments support accelerated liberalization by drawing up clear timetables and deadlines with practical measures to obtain this goal.

In this context, the 1993 Council Resolution remains a useful point of reference. Even before the specified dates, governments should take best advantage of its built-in flexibility to seize the opportunities offered by a burgeoning competitive market. They should speed up the opening to competition of infrastructures and of those services that are still in the monopoly area, as well as remove political burdens imposed on their national TOs.

Chapter 3: Completing the agenda

Several policy issues have to be faced in parallel with actions needed to create an open, competitive and market-driven information society. Disparate national regulatory reactions carry a very real threat of fragmentation to the internal market.

Here there are two different sets of issues and problems: one relating to the business community, the other more to individuals and the information society, with specific reference to privacy.

As we move into the information society, a regulatory response in key areas such as intellectual property, privacy and media ownership is required at the European level in order to maximize the benefits of the single market for all players. Only the scale of the internal market is sufficient to justify and attract the required financing of high performance trans-European information networks.

Therefore, applying the single market principle of freedom of movement of all goods and services, to the benefit of Europeans everywhere, must be our key objective.

> **The information society is global. The group thus recommends that Union action should aim to establish a common and agreed regulatory framework for the protection of intellectual property rights, privacy and security of information, in Europe and, where appropriate internationally.**

Protection of intellectual property rights (IPR)

While there is a great deal of information that is in the public domain, there is also information containing added value which is proprietary and needs protection via the enforcement of intellectual property rights. IPRs are an important factor in developing a competitive European industry, both in the area of information technology and more generally across a wide variety of industrial and cultural sectors.

> **The group believes that intellectual property protection must rise to the new challenges of globalization and multimedia and must continue to have a high priority at both European and international levels.**

Creativity and innovation are two of the Union's most important assets. Their protection must continue to be a high priority, on the basis of balanced solutions which do not impede the operation of market forces.

The global nature of the services that will be provided through the information networks means that the Union will have to be party to international action to protect intellectual property. Otherwise, serious difficulties will arise if regulatory systems in different areas of the world are operating on incompatible principles which permit circumvention or create jurisdictional uncertainties.

In this global information market-place, common rules must be agreed and enforced by everyone. Europe has a vested interest in ensuring that protection of IPRs receives full attention and that a high level of protection is maintained. Moreover, as the technology advances, regular world-wide consultation with all interested parties, both the suppliers and the user communities, will be required.

Initiatives already under way within Europe, such as the proposed Directive on the legal protection of electronic databases, should be completed as a matter of priority.

Meanwhile, in order to stimulate the development of new multimedia products and services, existing legal regimes — both national and Union — will have to be reexamined to see whether they are appropriate to the new information society. Where necessary, adjustments will have to be made.

In particular, the ease with which digitized information can be transmitted, manipulated and adapted requires solutions protecting the content providers. But, at the same time, flexibility and efficiency in obtaining authorization for the exploitation of works will be a prerequisite for a dynamic European multimedia industry.

Privacy

The demand for the protection of privacy will rightly increase as the potential of the new technologies to secure (even across national frontiers) and to manipulate detailed information on individuals from data, voice and image sources is realized. Without the legal security of a Union-wide approach, lack of consumer confidence will certainly undermine rapid development of the information society.

Europe leads the world in the protection of the fundamental rights of the individual with regard to personal data processing. The application of new technologies potentially affects highly sensitive areas such as those dealing with the images of individuals, their communication, their movements and their behaviour. With this in mind, it is quite possible that most Member States will react to these developments by adopting protection, including trans-frontier control of new technologies and services.

Disparities in the level of protection of such privacy rules create the risk that national authorities might restrict free circulation of a wide range of new services between Member States in order to protect personal data.

> **The group believes that without the legal security of a Union-wide approach, lack of consumer confidence will certainly undermine the rapid development of the information society. Given the importance and sensitivity of the privacy issue, a fast decision from Member States is required on the Commission's proposed Directive setting out general principles of data protection.**

Electronic protection (encryption), legal protection and security

Encryption is going to become increasingly important in assuring the development of the pay services. Encryption will ensure that only those who pay will receive the service. It will also provide protection against personal data falling into the public domain.

International harmonization would assist the market if it were to lead to a standard system of scrambling. Conditional access should ensure fair and open competition in the interests of consumers and service providers.

Encryption is particularly important for tele-commerce, which requires absolute guarantees

in areas such as the integrity of signatures and text, irrevocable time and date-stamping and international legal recognition.

However, the increased use of encryption and the development of a single encryption system will increase the returns from hacking into the system to avoid payment or privacy restrictions. Without a legal framework that would secure service providers against piracy of their encryption system, there is the risk that they will not get involved in the development of these new services.

> **The group recommends acceleration of work at European level on electronic and legal protection as well as security.**

On the other hand, governments may need powers to override encryption for the purposes of fighting against crime and protecting national security.

An answer given at a national level to this and to the hacking issue will inevitably prove to be insufficient because communications reach beyond national frontiers and because the principles of the internal market prohibit measures such as import bans on decoding equipment.

Therefore, a solution at the European level is needed which provides a global answer to the problem of protection of encrypted signals and security. Based on the principles of the internal market it would create parity of conditions for the protection of encrypted services as well as the legal framework for the development of these new services.

Media ownership

In addition to ownership controls to prevent monopoly abuse, most countries have rules on media and cross media ownership to preserve pluralism and freedom of expression.

In practice, these rules are a patchwork of inconsistency which tend to distort and fragment the market. They impede companies from taking advantage of the opportunities offered by the internal market, especially in multimedia, and could put them in jeopardy vis-à-vis non-European competitors.

In current circumstances, there is a risk of each Member State adopting purely national legislation in response to the new problems and challenges posed by the information society. Urgent attention has to be given to the question of how we can avoid such an undermining of the internal market and ensure effective rules which protect pluralism and competition.

Rules at the European level are going to be crucial, given the universality of the information society and its inherently transborder nature. The Union will have to lead the way in heading off deeper regulatory disparity. In so doing it will reinforce the legal security that is vital for the global competitiveness of Europe's media industry.

> **The group believes that urgent attention should be given to the question of how we can avoid divergent national legislation on media ownership undermining the internal market. Effective rules must emerge to protect pluralism and competition.**

The role of competition policy

Competition policy is a key element in Union strategy. It is especially important for consolidating the single market and for attracting the private capital necessary for the growth of the trans-European information infrastructure.

Areas of the information society are beset by intense globalizing pressures. These affect both European and non-European companies operating inside the Union. If appropriate, the notion of a global, rather than a Union-wide, market should now be used in assessing European competition issues such market power, joint ventures and alliances.

The aim should not be to freeze any set of regulations, but rather to establish procedures and policies through which the exploding dynamism of the sector can be translated into greater opportunities for wealth and job creation.

Like other commercial players, companies involved in the supply of technologies and services must be in a position to adapt their strategies and to forge alliances to enable them to contribute to, and to benefit from, overall growth in the sector in the framework of competition policy.

> **Competition policy is a key element in Europe's strategy. The group recommends that the application of competition rules should reflect the reality of the newly emerging global markets and the speed of change in the environment.**

Technology

The technological base in Europe today is sufficient, to launch the applications proposed in this report without delay. They must focus on realistic systems on a sufficient scale to explore the value of the services offered to the user, and to evaluate the economic feasibility of the new information systems.

However, new technologies do still have to be developed for their full-scale introduction following these demonstrations. In particular, the usability and cost-effectiveness of the systems must be improved, and the consequences of mass use further investigated.

The research programmes of the Union and of Member States, in particular the Fourth Framework Programme, should be implemented in such a way as to take into account market requirements. Technical targets and the timing of projects must be defined with appropriate user involvement.

Chapter 4: The building blocks of the information society

Communications systems combined with advanced information technologies are keys to the information society. The constraints of time and distance have been removed by networks (e.g. telephone, satellites, cables) which carry the information, basic services (e.g. electronic mail, interactive video) which allow people to use the networks and applications (e.g. distance learning, teleworking) which offer dedicated solutions for user groups.

The opportunity for the Union — strengthening its existing networks and accelerating the creation of new ones

ISDN: a first step

The traditional telephone network is changing its character. Having been built as a universal carrier for voice, it now has to meet the communication requirements of a modern economy going far beyond simple telephone calls.

One important development is the integrated service digital network ISDN. This offers the opportunity to send not only voice, but also data and even moving images through telephone lines.

ISDN is particularly suited for the communications needs of small and medium-sized enterprises. It permits, for example, direct PC to PC communication, for the instant, low-cost transmission of documents. Teleworking using ISDN services can be attractive to a wide range of businesses. ISDN is also an ideal support for distance learning.

EURO-ISDN, based on common standards, started at the end of 1993. A number of European countries have a leading position which should be exploited.

> **The group recommends priority extension of the availability of EURO-ISDN, in line with current Commission proposals, and reductions in tariffs to foster the market.**

Broadband: the path to multimedia

ISDN is only the first step. New multimedia services, for instance high-quality video communications, require even more performance. ISDN is showing the way, and the next technological wave aims for the multimedia-world. This is integrated broadband communications, providing an opportunity to combine all media in a flexible way. The lead technology to implement this is called asynchronous transfer mode (ATM).

European industry and telecoms operators are at the forefront of these technological developments and should reap the benefits.

Europe needs to develop an ATM broadband infrastructure as the backbone of the information society. Multimedia services offered through these networks will support the work and leisure activities of all our citizens.

In many European countries, highly developed broadband distribution already exists in the form of cable and satellite networks, or is being deployed. The application of currently available sophisticated digital techniques, such as picture compression and digital signal transmission, will easily enable these networks to fulfil mainstream demands for interactive individual information and leisure uses.

The present situation is mainly characterized by national and regional initiatives. The first trials of transnational networks have only recently taken place.

> **The group recommends that the Council supports the implementation of the European broadband infrastructure and secures its interconnectivity with the whole of European telecom, cable television and satellite networks.**
>
> **A European broadband steering committee involving all relevant actors should be set up in order to develop a common vision and to monitor and facilitate the realization of the overall concept through, in particular, demonstrations and choice and definition of standards.**

Mobile communication: a growing field

Mobile communication is growing at breathtaking speed. The number of mobile telephone subscribers has doubled over the past three years to 8 million. At current growth rates of 30 to 40%, the Union will soon have 40 million users.

Europe is becoming an important leader in mobile communications through adoption around the world of its standards for digital communications. In particular, GSM is an excellent demonstration of how a common Europe-wide public/private initiative can be successfully transformed into a market driven, job-creating operation.

In Germany, the country where GSM is currently having most success, about 30 000 new jobs have been created. On similar assumptions, Europe-wide introduction on the same scale would generate more than 100 000 new jobs.

Satellites: widening the scope of communications

Satellites are mainly used for television broadcasting, Earth observation and telecommunications. The crucial advantage of satellites is their wide geographical coverage without the need for expensive terrestrial networks. Satellites have many advantages for providing rural and remote areas with advanced communications.

Full exploitation of satellites can only be achieved by a new phase in the Union's satellite policy. The objective should be to develop trans-European networks.

> **With regard to mobile and satellite communications, the group recommends:**
>
> - **a reduction in tariffs for mobile communications;**
> - **promotion of GSM, in Europe and internationally;**
> - **the establishment of a regulatory framework for satellite communications;**
> - **urging the European satellite industry to develop common priority projects and to participate actively in the development of worldwide systems.**

New basic services are needed

New basic services such as E-mail, file transfer and interactive multimedia are needed. The necessary technology is available. New networks are developing, such as ISDN, eliminating the present limitations of the telephone network.

Two basic elements are needed for such services: unambiguous standards and critical mass. The attraction of a telecommunications service depends directly on the number of other compatible users. Thus, a new service cannot really take off until a certain number of customers have subscribed to the service. Once this critical mass has been achieved, growth rates can increase dramatically, as in the case of Internet.

Internet is based on a world-wide network of networks that is not centrally planned. In fact, nobody owns Internet. There are now some 20 million users in more than 100 countries. The network offers electronic mail, discussion forums, information exchange and much more. Internet is so big, and growing so fast, that it cannot be ignored. Nevertheless, it has flaws, notably serious security problems. Rather than remaining merely clients, we in Europe should consider following the evolution of Internet closely, playing a more active role in the development of interlinkages.

> **The group recommends urgent and coherent action at both European and Member State levels to promote the provision and widespread use of standard, trans-European basic services, including electronic mail, file transfer and video services.**
>
> **The Commission is recommended to initiate the creation of a 'European basic services forum' to accelerate the availability of unified standards for basic services.**

Significant advantages for the whole economy could be realized quite quickly through extension of Europe-wide compatible basic services.

Blazing the trail — ten applications to launch the information society

Today technology is in search of applications. At the same time, societies are searching for solutions to problems based on intelligent information.

Tariff reductions will facilitate the creation of new applications and so overcome the present low rate of capacity utilization. Voicelines operate, for instance, an average of 20 minutes in 24 hours, while some value-added network services are only working at 20% of capacity.

However, confident as we are of the necessity to liberate market forces, heightened competition will not produce by itself, or will produce too slowly, the critical mass which has the power to drive investment in new networks and services.

We can only create a virtuous circle of supply and demand if a significant number of market testing applications based on information networks and services can be launched across Europe to create critical mass.

Demonstration function

Initiatives taking the form of experimental applications are the most effective means of addressing the slow take-off of demand and supply. They have a demonstration function which would help to promote their wider use; they provide an early test bed for suppliers to fine-tune applications to customer requirements, and they can stimulate advanced users, still relatively few in number in Europe as compared to the US.

It is necessary to involve local, metropolitan and regional administrations in their development. Cities can have an extremely important role in generating early demand and also in promoting an awareness among their citizens of the advantages of the new services. In certain cases, local administrations could demonstrate the benefits by assuming the role of the first mass user.

To be truly effective, such applications need to be launched in real commercial environments, preferably on a large scale. These initiatives are not pilot projects in the traditional sense. The first objective is to test the value to the user, and the second, the economic feasibility of the information systems.

As the examples on the following pages demonstrate, it is possible to identify initiatives which will rapidly develop new applications and markets, while also having a positive impact on the creation of new jobs and businesses.

The private sector is ready to embark on the initiatives needed.

Priority applications can be divided into two main blocks, according to final users:

☐ the personal home market (interactive and transaction applications related to teleshopping, telebanking, entertainment and leisure)

☐ business and social applications.

Priority applications should also contribute to a number of macroeconomic objectives:

☐ strengthening industrial competitiveness and promoting the creation of new jobs

☐ promoting new forms of work organization

☐ improving quality of life and the quality of the environment

☐ responding to social needs and raising the efficiency and cost-effectiveness of public services.

Application one
TELEWORKING
More jobs, new jobs, for a mobile society

What should be done? Promote teleworking in homes and satellite offices so that commuters no longer need to travel long distances to work. From there, they can connect electronically to whatever professional environment they need, irrespective of the system in use.

Who will do it? If the telecom operators make available the required networks at competitive prices, the private sector will set up new service companies to supply teleworking support.

Who gains? Companies (both large and SMEs) and public administrations will benefit from productivity gains, increased flexibility and cost savings. For the general public, pollution levels, traffic congestion and energy consumption will be reduced. For employees, more flexible working arrangements will be particularly beneficial for all those tied to the home, and for people in remote locations the narrowing of distances will help cohesion.

Issues to watch? Problems arising from decreased opportunities for social contact and promotion will have to be addressed. Impact on labour legislation and social security provision will need to be assessed.

What target? Create pilot teleworking centres in 20 cities by end 1995 involving at least 20 000 workers. The aim is for 2% of white collar workers to be teleworkers by 1996; 10 million teleworking jobs by the year 2000.

Application two
DISTANCE LEARNING
Lifelong learning for a changing society

What should be done? Promote distance learning centres providing courses, training and tuition services tailored for SMEs, large companies and public administrations. Extend advanced distance learning techniques into schools and colleges.

Who will do it? Given the required network tariffs at competitive prices, industry will set up new service-provider companies to supply distance learning services for vocational training. The European Commission should support quality standards for programmes and courses and help create a favourable environment. Private sector providers and public authorities will enter the distance education market, offering networked and CD-I and CD-ROM interactive disk based programming and content at affordable prices.

Who gains? Industry (specially SMEs) and public administrations, by cost reductions and optimization of the use of scarce training and education resources. Employees needing to upgrade their skills by taking advantage of lifelong learning programmes. People tied to the home and in remote locations. Students accessing higher quality teaching.

Issues to watch? Need to engage in a major effort to train the trainers and expand computer literacy among the teaching profession.

What target? Pilot projects in at least 5 countries by 1995. Distance learning in use by 10% of SMEs and public administrations by 1996. Awareness campaigns among the professional associations and education authorities.

Application three
A NETWORK FOR UNIVERSITIES AND RESEARCH CENTRES
Networking Europe's brain power

What should be done? Development of a trans-European advanced network (high bandwidth, high definition, carrying interactive multimedia services) linking universities and research centres across Europe, with open access to their libraries.

Who will do it? Providing broadband networks and high speed lines are available at competitive rates, universities and research centres will set up the networks. Private companies, large and small, could also link their laboratories with universities and research centres. A trans-European public library network can also be envisaged.

Who gains? The productivity of research programmes through broader team creation leading to synergies between institutions. Society in general through more efficient diffusion of research findings and knowledge.

Issues to watch? Giving due consideration to IPR protection as the accumulated stock of human knowledge becomes more readily accessible.

What target? Thirty per cent of European universities and research centres linked through advanced communications networks by 1997. Extension to other European countries as this becomes technologically feasible.

Application four
TELEMATIC SERVICES FOR SMEs
Relaunching a main engine for growth and employment in Europe

What should be done? Promote the widest possible use of telematic services (E-mail), file transfer, EDI, video conferencing, distance learning, etc.) by European SMEs, with links to public authorities, trade associations, customers and suppliers. Raise the awareness of value-added services, and communications in general, among SMEs. Increase access to trans-European data networks.

Who will do it? If the necessary ISDN networks are available at competitive rates, the private sector will provide trans-European value-added services tailored for SMEs. Local government, chambers of commerce and trades associations linking SMEs will mount programmes for integrating information networks at local and regional level, promoting awareness campaigns for the services available.

Who gains? SMEs will be able to compete on a more equal basis with larger companies and captive contractor-supplier relationships will be weakened. They will be more competitive, will grow faster and create more jobs. Relationships with administrations will be simpler and more productive. The category will gain in public standing and influence.

What target? Access to trans-European telematic services for SMEs available by end 1994–95. In all 40% of SMEs (firms with more than 50 employees) using telematic networks by 1996. SME links with administration networks prioritized.

Application five

ROAD TRAFFIC MANAGEMENT
Electronic roads for better quality of life

What should be done? Establish telematic solutions on a European scale for advanced road traffic management systems and other transport services (driver information, route guidance, fleet management, road pricing, etc.).

Who will do it? European, national and regional administrations, user groups and traffic operators will create a steering committee and define a common open-system architecture for advanced telematic services with common user interfaces.

Who gains? Drivers, local communities (especially in heavily congested areas) and industry will benefit from reduction in traffic, increased road safety, lower environmental costs, energy and time saving.

What target? Implementation of telematic systems for road traffic management in 10 metropolitan areas and 2 000 km of motorway by 1996. Implementation in 30 metropolitan areas and the trans-European motorway network by the year 2000.

Application six

AIR TRAFFIC CONTROL
An electronic airway for Europe

What should be done? Create a European air traffic communication system providing ground to ground connections between all European air traffic control centres (ATC) and air to ground connections between aeroplanes, ATC-centres across the European Union and the European civil aviation conference, with the aim of achieving a unified trans-European air traffic control system.

Who will do it? The European Council should promote energetically the creation of a reduced number of networked European air traffic centres, as defined by Eurocontrol.

Who gains? The European air transport industry — and its millions of passengers — will benefit

from better air traffic management and significantly reduced energy consumption. A safer system, with less congestion and subsequent reductions in time wasted, noise and fume pollution.

Issues to watch? There is a need to coordinate closely with the defence sector.

What target? Set up a steering committee with representatives of public authorities, civil and military aviation authorities, the air transport industry and unions by end 1994. Definition of standards for communication procedures and the exchange of data and voice messages between ATC-centres as well as between ATC-centres and aeroplanes. A functioning trans-European system before the year 2000.

Application seven
HEALTHCARE NETWORKS
Less costly and more effective healthcare systems for Europe's citizens

What should be done? Create a direct communication 'network of networks' based on common standards linking general practitioners, hospitals and social centres on a European scale.

Who will do it? The private sector, insurance companies, medical associations and Member State healthcare systems, with the European Union promoting standards and portable applications. Once telecom operators make available the required networks at reduced rates, the private sector will create competitively priced services at a European level, boosting the productivity and cost effectiveness of the whole healthcare sector.

Who gains? Citizens as patients will benefit from a substantial improvement in healthcare (improve-ment in diagnosis through on-line access to European specialists, on-line reservation of analysis and hospital services by practitioners extended on European scale, transplant matching, etc.). Taxpayers and public administrations will benefit from tighter cost control and cost savings in healthcare spending and a speeding up of reimbursement procedures.

Issues to watch? Privacy and the confidentiality of medical records will need to be safeguarded.

What target? Major private sector health care providers linked on a European scale. First-level implementation of networks in Member States linking general practitioners, specialists and hospitals at a regional and national level by end 1995.

Application eight
ELECTRONIC TENDERING
More effective administration at a lower cost

What should be done? Introduction of electronic procedures for public procurement between public administrations and suppliers in Europe followed by the creation of a European electronic tendering network. This programme will function as a strong enabling mechanism for attaining critical mass in the telematic services market in Europe.

Who will do it? European Council and Member States decide to agree on common standards and to introduce a mandatory commitment to electronic handling of information, bidding and payments related to public procurement. Telecom operators and service providers will enable users to access to the European electronic tendering network.

Who gains? Public administrations will benefit from cost savings in replacing paper handling with electronic handling and from the more competitive environment between suppliers drawn from the wider internal market. Small and medium-sized enterprises will benefit from participating in trans-European public procurement and from the diffusion of telematic services.

Issues to watch? Data security, the need to ensure open access particularly for SMEs, to avoid electronic procurement developing into a hidden form of protectionism. Take proper account of similar programmes developed in third countries, particularly the US (CALS).

What target? A critical mass of 10% of awarding authorities using electronic procedures for their procurement needs could be attained in the next two to three years.

Application nine

TRANS-EUROPEAN PUBLIC ADMINISTRATION NETWORK
Better government, cheaper government

What should be done? Interconnected networks between public administrations' networks in Europe, aiming at providing an effective and less expensive (replacement of paper by electronic means) information interchange. Subsequently extended to link public administrations and European citizens.

Who will do it? European Union and Member States should strengthen and speed up the implementation of the programme for interchange of data between administrations (IDA). The private sector will increase its cooperation with the European Union and Member States in defining technical solutions for the provision of interoperable services and interconnectable networks, while supporting national and local authorities in the testing and implementation of networks and services for citizens.

Who gains? The unification process for the single market, with general benefits in lower costs and better relations between public administrations and European citizens.

What target? Implementation of interconnected networks allowing interchange in the tax, customs and excise, statistical, social security, health care domains, etc., by 1995–96.

Application ten

CITY INFORMATION HIGHWAYS
Bringing the information society into the home

What should be done? Set up networks providing households with a network access system and the means of using on-line multimedia and entertainment services on a local, regional, national and international basis.

Who will do it? Groups of content and service providers (broadcasters, publishers), network operators (telecoms organizations, cable), system suppliers/integrators (e.g. consumer electronic industry). Local and regional authorities, citizens' groups and chambers of commerce and industry, will have very important roles to play.

Who gains? Consumers will enjoy early experience of complex new services, particulary multimedia services, and will be able to express their preferences in the fields of entertainment (video on demand), transaction-oriented services (banking, home shopping etc.) as well as gaining access to information services and teleworking or telelearning.

Public authorities will gain experience with issues such as privacy, IPR protection and standardization which will be helpful in defining a single legal and regulatory environment.

Private sector participants will gain early hands-on experience of consumer preferences for programmes, software and services. User interfaces can be tested and improved in practice.

What target? Install and operate in up to five European cities with up to 40 000 households per city by 1997.

Chapter 5: Financing the information society — a task for the private sector

It is neither possible nor necessary at this stage to be precise about the amount of investment that will be generated by the development of the information infrastructure and related services and applications. Analyses made of the US market remain highly questionable, although there is no doubt that the total investment required over the next 5 to 10 years will be considerable.

The group believes the creation of the information society in Europe should be entrusted to the private sector and to market forces.

Private capital will be available to fund new telecoms services and infrastructures providing that the different elements of this report's action plan are implemented so that:

☐ market liberalization is fast and credible
☐ rules for interoperability and reciprocal access are set
☐ tariffs are adjusted
☐ the regulatory framework is established.

There will be no need for public subsidies, because sufficient confidence will have been established to attract the required investment from private sources.

Ultimately, it is market growth that is perceived as the real guarantee for private investors, rendering subsidies and monopolies superfluous.

Public investment will assume a role, but not by any increase in the general level of public spending — rather by a refocusing of existing expenditure. Indeed, some of the investment that public authorities will have to undertake to develop applications in areas of their own responsibility will generate productivity gains and an improvement in the quality of services that should, if properly handled, lead to savings.

In addition to some refocusing of expenditure on R&D, modest amounts of public money may also be useful to support awareness campaigns mainly directed at small and medium-sized businesses and individual consumers.

The group recommends refocusing existing public funding more specifically to target the requirements of the information society. At Union level, this may require some reorientation of current allocations under such headings as the Fourth Framework Programme for research and development and the Structural Funds.

The same is true for expenditure at the European Union which can achieve important results by a better focusing of existing resources, including finance available under both the Fourth Framework Programme funding R&D, and under the Structural Funds.

The Commission has also proposed limited support for some of the services and applications included in the group's action plan from funds linked to the promotion of trans-European networks. These proposals deserve support.

Chapter 6: Follow-up

With this report the group has completed its mandate and provided recommendations for action. Our recommendations should be regarded as a coherent whole, the full benefits of which can only be reaped if action is taken in all areas.

Given the urgency and importance of the tasks ahead, the group believes that at Union level there must be one Council capable of dealing with the full range of issues associated with the information society. With this in mind, each Member State may wish to nominate a single minister to represent it in a Council of Ministers dedicated to the information society. The Commission should act similarly.

The group calls for the establishment by the Commission of a Board composed of eminent figures from all sectors concerned, including the social partners, to work on the framework for implementing the information society and to promote public awareness of its opportunities and challenges. This Board should report at regular intervals to the institutions of the Union on progress made on the implementation of the recommendations contained in this report.

An action plan — summary of recommendations

Regulatory framework

Evolving the regulatory domain

Member States should accelerate the ongoing process of liberalization of the telecom sector by:

- opening up to competition infrastructures and services still in the monopoly area
- removing non-commercial political burdens and budgetary constraints imposed on telecommunications operators
- setting clear timetables and deadlines for the implementation of practical measures to achieve these goals.

An authority should be established at European level whose terms of reference will require prompt attention.

Interconnection and interoperability

Interconnection of networks and interoperability of services and applications should be primary Union objectives. The European standardization process should be reviewed in order to increase its speed and responsiveness to markets.

Tariffs

As a matter of urgency the international, long distance and leased-line tariffs should be adjusted to bring these down into line with rates practised in other advanced industrialized regions. The adjustment should be accompanied by the fair-sharing of public service obligations among operators.

Critical mass

Public awareness should be promoted. Particular attention should be paid to the small and medium-sized business sector, public administrations and the younger generation.

Worldwide dimension

The openness of the European market should find its counterpart in markets and networks of other regions of the world. It is of paramount importance for Europe that adequate steps should be taken to guarantee equal access.

Completing the agenda

The information society is global.
Union action should aim to establish a common and agreed regulatory framework for the protection of intellectual property rights, privacy and security of information in Europe and, where appropriate, internationally.

IPRs

Intellectual property protection must rise to the new challenges of globalization and multimedia, and must continue to have a high priority at both European and international levels.

Privacy

Without the legal security of a Union-wide approach, lack of consumer confidence will certainly undermine the rapid development of the information society. Given the importance and sensitivity of the privacy issue, a fast decision from Member States is required on the Commission's proposed Directive setting out general principles of data protection.

Electronic protection, legal protection and security

Work at the European level on electronic and legal protection as well as security should be accelerated.

Media ownership

Urgent attention should be given to the question of how we can avoid divergent national legislation on media ownership undermining the internal market. Effective rules must emerge to protect pluralism and competition.

Competition

Competition is a key element in Europe's strategy. The application of competition rules should reflect the reality of the newly emerging global markets and the speed of change in the environment.

Building blocks

Networks

Priority has to be given to the extension of the availability of EURO-ISDN, in line with current Commission proposals, and reductions in tariffs to foster the market.

The Council should support the implementation of the European broadband infrastructure and secure its interconnectivity with the whole of European telecom, cable television and satellite networks.

A European broadband steering committee involving all relevant actors should be set up in order to develop a common vision and to monitor and facilitate the realization of the overall concept through, in particular, demonstrations, and choice and definition of standards.

With regard to mobile and satellite communications:
- tariffs for mobile communications should be reduced
- GSM should be promoted in Europe and internationally
- a regulatory framework for satellite communications should be established
- the European satellite industry should be urged to develop common priority projects and to participate actively in the development of world-wide systems.

Basic services

The provision and widespread use of standard trans-European basic services, including electronic mail, file transfer and video services, should be promoted by urgent and coherent action at both European and Member State level.

The Commission should initiate the creation of a 'European basic services forum' to accelerate the availability of unified standards for basic services.

Applications

Initiatives in the application domain are the most effective means of addressing the slow take-off of demand and supply. They have a demonstration function which would help promoting their use. The group has identified the following initiatives:

- Teleworking
- Distance learning
- University and research networks
- Telematic services for SMEs
- Road traffic management
- Air traffic control
- Healthcare networks
- Electronic tendering
- Trans-European public administration network
- City information highways.

Financing

The creation of the information society should be entrusted to the private sector and to the market forces.

The existing public funding should be refocused more specifically to target the requirements of the information society. At Union level, this may require some reorientation of current allocations under such headings as the Fourth Framework Programme for research and development and the Structural Funds.

Follow-up

Given the urgency and importance of the tasks ahead, there must be, at Union level, one Council capable of dealing with the full range of issues associated with the information society. With this in mind, each Member State may wish to nominate a single minister to represent it in a Council of Ministers dedicated to the information society. The Commission should act similarly.

A board composed of eminent figures from all sectors concerned, including the social partners, should be established by the Commission to work on the framework for implementing the information society and to promote public awareness of its opportunities and challenges. This board should report at regular intervals to the institutions of the Union on progress made on the implementation of the recommendations contained in this report.

Trans-European networks

Interim report of the chairman of the group of personal representatives of the Heads of State or Government to the Corfu European Council
(Christophersen group)

Contents

Foreword

The European Council in December 1993 invited the Commission, assisted by a group of personal representatives of the Heads of State or Government, to lead and coordinate the speedy and efficient implementation of trans-European networks in transport and energy.

In presenting, on behalf of the Commission, this interim report on the work of the group of personal representatives, I am pleased first of all to convey my personal conviction that the implementation of trans-European networks is gathering momentum.

The task that the Union and the Member States have undertaken consists first of all in identifying and accelerating projects considered to be of priority importance.

Secondly, the task involves improving conditions for implementation of trans-European networks in the future, i.e. creating better conditions in the regulatory frameworks and for attracting private financing. In this sense, the task has the wider objective of creating structural improvements of a permanent nature.

In both areas, there are prospects for significant progress. While it is true that large infrastructure projects inevitably take a long time to prepare, launch and complete, it can already now be stated that the work initiated simultaneously in Member States, at the Union level in a broad sense and among private operators has clear and positive synergy effects. In this respect, the group has made a significant contribution.

Considerable work still needs to be done, mainly in the fields of the regulatory framework and financing. Furthermore, I would like to emphasize the high priority attached by the group to the question of extending the trans-European networks towards third countries.

The report is intended to give an account of the proceedings of the group up to its last meeting on 3 June 1994, as well as a brief description of the two main areas of importance for the implementation of large infrastructure projects, i.e. the regulatory framework and financing.

The interim report is drawn up on the chairman's responsibility. It has, however, met with broad consensus among the group members.

In addition, the group has drawn up the following common conclusions.

Henning CHRISTOPHERSEN

Conclusions

In view of the results of the work of the group of personal representatives in identifying priority projects of Community interest and without prejudging the future work of the group in this respect, the European Council is invited to:

☐ acknowledge the priority status for the European Community of the list of transport projects so far identified by the group (Appendix 2), provided they continue to meet the economic viability and other criteria on which the projects have been selected;

☐ take note of the list of priority energy projects (Appendix 4) which is still subject to further examination by the group;

☐ recommend to the Member States that they facilitate the implementation of these projects by accelerating the administrative, regulatory and legal procedures and processes that are at present delaying them.

The group of personal representatives has made significant progress in carrying out the task given to it by the European Council at its meeting in Brussels in December 1993. Its work however is not yet finished. It is therefore further proposed to the European Council to confirm the mandate of the group until the Essen European Council and to instruct it in particular to:

☐ complete the assessment of the projects and their priority status taking full advantage of the professional input of the EIB in order to establish a final list;

☐ facilitate and monitor the work of the project seminars convened by the European Commission, with the full involvement of the EIB, gathering, as appropriate, interested parties, both public and private; assist the Commission in appraising the most appropriate ways and means to respond effectively to the problems identified as holding up full realization of individual projects;

☐ study the problems arising from the regulatory framework, both at Community level and in Member States with a view to overcoming or alleviating administrative obstacles;

☐ assessing, taking full advantage of EIB expertise and the findings of the project seminars, appropriate forms of financial engineering encouraging the participation of the private sector whenever possible;

☐ contribute to the assessment of financial needs and instruments according to the timescales and the financing plans of the identified priority projects;

☐ study further the extension of the TENs to neighbouring countries, in particular to Central and East European countries and the Mediterranean Basin.

Part one: Work under way

The political context

The trans-European networks (TENs) have recently received increasing attention. This is reflected in the growing references to them in the conclusions of past European Councils and in the Treaty of European Union, Title XII. In its White Paper 'Growth, Competitiveness, Employment' the Commission proposed the acceleration of the trans-European networks as one of the major development themes. The European Council last December confirmed this approach and took a series of important decisions aimed at accelerating the implementation of the TEN. One of these decisions was to create a special group of personal representatives of Heads of State or Government to assist the Commission in its task as regards transport and energy network infrastructures. The work of this group and the present interim report are to be seen in this general political context.

As a result of the foregoing, the general public, the media, national and regional administrations, interested industrial and financial operators have shown increasing interest in TENs, on the need for their implementation and on the Union's determination to speed up and facilitate their development.

lp;&-4dFurthermore, a favourable climate for partnership between Member States, the Union's institutions, the world of business and banking and operators is developing. The Union has made it clear that it welcomes the emergence of partnerships between the private and the public sector in the realization of TENs.

The Commission's White Paper provides the background for the importance of TENs to competitiveness, and hence to growth and employment.

The Action Plan agreed at the meeting of the European Council in December includes specific action to be taken by the Union and the Member States on trans-European networks. The overall objective is the speedy completion of the TENs with a view to the efficient operation of the single market; to reinforcing the Union's competitiveness, regional planning and the links with neighbouring countries; and to contributing to faster and safer means of communication for the citizen.

The White Paper also outlines some of the obstacles to the implementation of TENs.

☐ The constraints on the Community's and the Member States' public budgets limit the scope of investment by the public sector.

☐ The long-term investment required in some sectors, particularly in transport infrastructures, necessitates new types of partnerships between private and public financing.

☐ The absence of open and competitive markets is hampering, to differing degrees, the optional use of existing networks and their completion in the interest both of consumers and operators.

☐ The inherent sluggishness of the preparation, planning, authorization and evaluation procedures and regulatory obstacles hamper the implementation of large projects.

Furthermore, experience shows that transnational projects frequently run into difficulties because of conflicting priorities between the countries involved.

Recent developments

It is important to stress that the Union is already actively involved in implementing trans-European networks.

Pursuant to Article 129 C of the Treaty and to the conclusions of the December European Council, the Commission has in the course of the first six months of 1994 tabled proposals for:

☐ guidelines in the fields of energy and transport; [1]

☐ high-speed trains interoperability;[2]

☐ a financial regulation for TENs.[3]

As regards financing, the Union, principally through the European Investment Bank, the Structural Funds and the Cohesion Fund, is contributing in a very substantial way to the development of TENs. Over the past 12 months the Union has also taken the following new initiatives.

1. The Commission has put forward a proposal for financing TENs on the basis of Article 129 C of the Treaty which would make available an estimated ECU 2.4 billion (at current prices) over the 1994–99 period.

2. The Cohesion Fund is formally established and will commit nearly ECU 6.8 billion (at 1992 prices) to TEN-related transport projects in the eligible countries.

3. The revised Regional Fund regulations specify that it can contribute to the financing of TENs and at this stage it is calculated that it could invest about ECU 1.0 to 1.6 billion yearly in TEN projects in the eligible regions.

4. In the framework of the Edinburgh and Copenhagen initiatives, the EIB has committed almost the full amount of ECU 7 billion available to transport, energy and telecommunications projects of Community interest.

5. The European Investment Fund is operational as from June 1994 and will have a key role to play in facilitating the financing of projects.

6. The European Economic Area financial mechanism is being set up and will help finance TENs in the areas selected for assistance (the mechanism totals ECU 1.5 billion of loans and ECU 0.5 billion in grants for TEN, SME and environment projects).

7. Decision to use part of the PHARE programme resources in particular in conjunction with the EIB, to finance TENs in Central and East European countries.

Thus the Union is already actively involved in preparing to improve transport and energy links across its territory and beyond.

Areas where action is called for

The Heads of State or Government asked the Commission to report to it annually on the progress being made.

In December 1993 the European Council invited the Council of the Union to make full and rapid use of the possibilities offered by Article 129 B of the Treaty to accelerate the implementation of the TENs. The European Council further invited the Council of the Union and the Parliament jointly to speed up the legislative procedures in order to allow the adoption, before 1 July 1994, of the guidelines which were still outstanding. The group notes that the Commission has tabled the necessary proposals on energy guidelines and multimodal transport guidelines and that they are still under discussion in the Community institutions. The group also notes that the financial regulation required for action on TENs under Article 129 C, proposed by the Commission in March 1994, has not yet been given a first reading by the European Parliament and is being discussed in the framework of the Council.

The European Council also invited the Member States to prepare as quickly as possible the investment programmes to be integrated with the networks.

---

[1] COM(93) 685 and COM(94) 106 respectively.
[2] COM(94) 107.
[3] COM(94) 62.

Aims and working methods of the group

The group saw its task as primarily one of speeding up and facilitating the work already underway in the Union and Member States, so that clear decisions on priorities could be taken and projects implemented. It is an objective not to duplicate the work being done elsewhere, especially in the Council of the Union but to aim for adding value to the work on implementing TENs. Specifically the group set itself the aim of:

☐ identifying priority projects and facilitating the subsequent work in specific project seminars

☐ speeding up administrative procedures and eliminating obstacles;

☐ addressing the horizontal obstacles to implementation of TENs in terms of the regulatory framework and finance;

☐ facilitating rapid political agreement on the transport and energy guidelines.

The list of the personal representatives of State or Government is to be found in Appendix 1. In view of the long experience of the European Investment Bank in financing major infrastructure works, Vice-President Christophersen invited the President of the Bank, Sir Brian Unwin, to participate in the group. The Commission also invited the Bank to take part in the various project seminars and other preparatory meetings. Between January and June 1994, the group met six times, once a month, and had discussions with a wide range of representatives of international and private financial organizations and leading industrial figures. Over 40 working papers were submitted.

The group's work has followed a bottom-up approach. This is on the one hand due to, in some cases, the very incomplete information available about proposed priority projects which in turn is related to the degree of maturity of projects. On the other hand, the bottom-up approach was chosen to provide concrete information about specific obstacles in project implementation, on the basis of which generalizations about horizontal difficulties and remedies could be formed. It was agreed that the decisions should be taken on the basis of the broadest consensus possible, so as to give the group's proposals a maximum impact.

In the bottom-up approach the seminars or workshops on individual projects play a central role. Depending on the specifics of each individual project, they involve in principle all interested partners: national and regional authorities, promoters, financial institutions, industrialists, users, etc. Their task is to identify specific problems of each individual project — financing in general, private-sector investment in particular, non-financial obstacles, especially of a planning and administrative nature, etc. — and propose concrete solutions. The Commission's role is that of the catalyst, first of all in convening the seminars. The EIB participates in these seminars as a matter of course. The findings of the project seminars have an important role to play in enabling the group to address horizontal issues and the Commission and EIB to further study the financing issue.

The group concentrated its attention initially on the transport priority projects because these raised more problems and were relatively more mature than those in the energy sector. It also initiated the examination of the extension of the TENs to neighbouring countries, in particular to Central and Eastern Europe and the Mediterranean Basin.

The group will take into account in its future work the only recently published Report of the group of prominent people from the telecommunications sector, under the chairmanship of Commissioner Bangemann, to the extent that it is of relevance to its own work.

Transport networks

The group set itself the primary task of identifying priority projects. On the basis of criteria worked out with the EIB (see below), the group agreed on a list of projects set out in Appendix 2 deserving further detailed examination. The European Council is asked to acknowledge the priority status for the European Community of the list of transport projects so far identified by the group, provided they continue to meet the economic viability and other criteria on which the projects have been selected.

The list, it should be added, is not now closed and definitive. As circumstances evolve and as more detailed information becomes available, new projects could be added and existing projects dropped or their ranking changed. The Commission will continue to study and discuss with Member States the projects proposed by the personal representatives but not included in the list. Absence from the current list is not indicative of rejection.

The 34 projects are classified into three groups according to their degree of maturity. The first group consists of projects whose work is either already underway or could begin within two years (i.e., before the end of 1996). The second group comprises projects whose acceleration appears possible so that work could begin in two years time (i.e., as from 1997 onwards). The third and last group lists projects which appear likely to take more time before work can begin or which require further study.

The list as it stands seems to show a bias in favour of certain modes of transport. This is not deliberate. It reflects primarily that work is more advanced in certain transport modes than in others.

Soon after the Corfu European Council the Commission will submit proposals on projects which deal with the implementation of new technologies on a European-wide basis, i.e., those which relate to traffic management and which will improve the use of infrastructure for all modes of transport (land, sea and air):

☐ road traffic management system;
☐ air traffic management system;
☐ vessel traffic management system;
multimodal positioning system by satellites;
☐ pilot projects for a railway management system.

A brief description, with accompanying maps, of the 11 projects considered to be the most mature is to be found in Appendix 3. The attention given to these first 11 projects should not, however, detract from the importance of the other priority projects listed.

The list has been drawn up on the basis of the suggested list of priority projects presented in the Commission's White Paper and on the basis of Member States' priorities. All the projects in the list except one figure in the multimodal transport guidelines[1] put forward by the Commission in last April.[1] They have been the subject of detailed discussion with Member States. The one exception concerns the implementation of new advanced transport technologies (project No 33).

On the basis of proposals made by the Commission and in collaboration with the EIB, the group agreed on a set of selection criteria. Projects should:

☐ be of exceptional scale, bearing in mind the type of project and the relative size of the Member States directly concerned;

☐ be of common interest, contributing to the Union's transport network or facilitating connection between neighbouring countries;

☐ pass the test of economic viability, including improvements in the Union's competitiveness and technological performance;

☐ contribute to important Union objectives such as economic and social cohesion;

---

[1] COM(94) 106.

☐ allow scope for private investment;

☐ be mature, so that the projects can be implemented quickly;

☐ avoid public financing of infrastructure leading to distortion of competition contrary to the common interest;

☐ comply with the Union's legislation regarding the protection of the environment.

The Commission has already begun to organize project seminars, or at least preparatory meetings, on the priority projects, beginning with those in the most mature subgroup.

Energy networks

On the basis of working papers, agreed selection criteria, and of the information gathered in the project seminars, the group has drawn up a list of eight priority projects which need to be examined further (see Appendix 4 for the list and Appendix 5 for the description of the projects and accompanying maps). The European Council is asked to take note of these priority projects.

In proposing this list the group is highlighting projects needing special attention. The Commission recalls that there are also other projects which are important and mature and whose implementation is underway or which are less mature and whose commissioning is only foreseen towards the turn of the century or even later. The group has not attempted to identify these other projects. The group underlined that energy projects are usually financed by the sector itself without much help from public finance.

The strategic importance of developing interconnections between energy networks and completing them where they are missing is justified by the degree of their contribution to:

☐ security of energy supply;
☐ competitiveness of the economy;
☐ economic and social cohesion;
☐ the external relations dimension;
☐ the development of the internal energy market through the liberalization of the conditions of access to existing and new networks.

The Treaty, with its new Title XII, and the White Paper, with its list of over 60 projects which will be needed in the Union in order to meet increased demand for natural gas and increased exchanges of electricity in the coming ten years have confirmed this strategic importance.

The Council of Ministers at its meeting of 25 May 1994 reached political agreement on the Guidelines[1] for the development of energy networks. It is anticipated that the Energy Ministers will be able to adopt a common position on these Guidelines at their next meeting, after receiving the opinion of the European Parliament (codecision procedure) and having finalized the list of projects of common interest.

The nature of the energy networks and the problems they are facing are in some respects different from those in the transport sector. The main differences result from the following factors:

☐ there is more limited public budgetary involvement in the energy networks than in the transport networks;

☐ as a rule, customers pay for services so that the energy companies can be sure of their investments and can assume responsibility for them;

☐ in general, energy companies use their own funds and/or raise money on the capital market (bank loans, bonds, etc.).

In the energy networks, the main obstacles are of an administrative nature:

☐ delays in authorization procedures (often caused by long debates on environmental issues);

---

[1] Including the criteria for identifying projects of common interest and the broad lines of Community action in the field of TEN projects in energy.

☐ insufficient coordination;

☐ differences in the perception by the countries involved of the priority of a project;

☐ political risk elements in the case of projects related to certain third countries.

Once these obstacles are overcome, money can normally be raised to pay for the construction of the project. Nevertheless, financing problems do exist in some cases in the energy networks; this may be the case for projects in the peripheral regions of the EU where the profitability of this type of project is less than in the central regions despite their established potential economic viability.

Some personal representatives argued that in the case of energy networks linking the Union with third countries, it was essential to avoid subsidies which would put Community supplies of energy at a competitive disadvantage.

Notwithstanding the differences between the energy and the transport sectors, the method developed by the group for the transport projects (bottom-up analysis, project seminars, etc.) is also applicable to the energy sector.

The group agreed on the following selection criteria in order to find the most suitable projects in accordance with its mandate:

☐ the objectives, technical definitions and priorities laid down in the Energy guidelines agreed at the 25 May Energy Council;

☐ positive economic impact, including improvements in the Union's competitiveness and technological performance;

☐ significant size in relation to the energy market of the country(ies) concerned;

☐ advanced maturity (work could start within a period of 2 or 3 years);

☐ encountering administrative or other problems which could delay projects or even jeopardize their implementation.

Project seminars or preparatory meetings on six of the eight priority projects have already taken place and the results so far are encouraging.

Environment

The environment is not mentioned in Title XII of the Treaty concerning trans-European networks, and the European Council in December last year did not give the group a specific mandate to discuss it. On the other hand, the European Council did ask the Commission to include the environment in its proposals as regards financing the networks and, in the Commission's view, there are certain similarities between the transport and energy networks and the type of environment project that the Commission's White Paper called for (large-scale, transnational, network dimensions, etc.).

In view of these similarities the Commission thought it would be useful to take the same approach for the environment as had been adopted for transport and energy — identify priority projects, organize project seminars, etc.

To this end the Commission held several informal meetings with the Member States to define selection criteria and identify priority projects which could be put forward. On the basis of this the Commission presented a working paper to the group.

The group recognized the importance of the environmental problems raised and some personal representatives were very much in favour of the group studying environmental projects too. However, in view of the differences of opinion about the interpretation of the European Council's conclusions, it did not enter into a substantive discussion, concluding that it had at present no clear mandate to do so. The environmental aspects of TENs in transport and energy are, however, an integral part of the group's work.

Extending the networks to third countries

There is a general consensus in the group about the political and economic importance of extending the TENs to neighbouring countries, in particular Central and Eastern Europe and the Mediterranean Basin.

The list of priority projects approved by the group already contains several projects extending the networks beyond the present borders of the Union. Additional proposals will be made later.

The group had preliminary discussions on this subject, *inter alia* on the basis of the conclusions of the Pan-European Transport Conference held in Crete in March 1994. This Conference considered a three layered approach as a starting point for future work on coherent infrastructure development at pan-European level. These three layers consist of:

1. The long term perspective for pan-European development of common interest on the basis of the United Nations conventions on European infrastructure planning for road, rail and combined transport.

2. The priorities of common interest for medium term development (2010). TENs for the Union territory and priority multi-modal corridors towards Central and East European countries (see indicative maps in Appendix 3).

3. The short term priority projects of common interest located on layer 2, expected to be implemented within five years, to be selected on the basis of agreed operational criteria (only Central and Eastern Europe).

In this context it is worth recalling that the European Council in Copenhagen decided that up to 15% of the PHARE resources could be used for financing transport and energy investment projects. Subject to final approval in the PHARE management committee, up to ECU 100 million have been set aside in the 1994 budget for financing TEN projects in Central and East European countries. This amount will in practice be combined with funding from the EIB, the EBRD and the World Bank. In addition, the European Parliament allotted a proportion of the 1994 budget to facilitate cross-border cooperation, including transport projects. In addition, approximately ECU 50 million has been made available through the 1992–94 PHARE regional transport programmes for the elimination of the most serious border-crossing bottlenecks of international importance in Central and East European countries.

The list of priority projects in the energy sector includes new pipelines linking the Union to two of its main gas suppliers, namely Algeria and Russia, and this along new transit routes. In the electricity sector, the project linking the eastern und western parts of Denmark will furthermore add a supplementary link between the Scandinavian countries and the Continental West European countries.

The group proposes to pursue its study of this question with a view to making more specific recommendations to the Essen European Council.

Part two: The way ahead

Problems to be overcome

In the process of identifying priority projects and ways of accelerating them, a number of potential specific problems have emerged which merit further analysis. These fall into two broad categories:

☐ the regulatory framework
☐ financing of TENs.

Concerning the regulatory framework for the implementation of infrastructure, the group has noted a number of likely problem areas. However, no analysis has been conducted so far. In the Commission's view, it would also be relevant for the group to consider these issues in the further work.

On the issue of financing, the European Council in December 1993 invited the Ecofin Council, together with the Commission and the EIB, to study this issue. The Commission has, as part of this work, consulted the group and the EIB. The group, not least by way of providing information on the financing situation for priority projects, has contributed significantly to advancing this analysis. The Commission presented to the Council on 1 June 1994 a communication concerning the financing of trans-European networks. [1] In this, the Commission presents its preliminary assessment of the financing situation for TENs. Within the group different views were expressed about the Commission's assessment.

On the issue of financing as well as on the regulatory framework, further information will have to be collected through a pragmatic bottom-up approach before the importance for the implementation of trans-European networks can be precisely assessed. In the following sections, a brief outline is given of the two areas for the further study.

Regulatory framework

It should first of all be noted that the group has not yet had the opportunity to address the different problems discussed below, either in a horizontal way or as a result of the findings of the different project seminars. It would, however be relevant for the group to do so in a bottom-up approach in order to achieve more planning certainty and to accelerate the implementation of the projects.

Transport

A point of departure in analysing this sector would obviously be the Community's own regulatory framework and the general orientations of the existing Community transport policy framework. The common EC transport policy is guided by two main principles which give some general indications in this respect. The first element is the market-economy orientation of this policy with freedom for the traveller or shipper to choose the form of transport that suits them best. The second leading principle, which is established in Community decisions and policy communications, is that transport infrastructure costs shall be borne by the users to the maximum extent feasible. This principle is looked at as one key element to establish a fair competition between the different transport services which might lead to a shift of market shares between modes. In that context the principle enhances the possibility of private sector commitment by enabling project-related revenues.

The development of trans-European transport infrastructure networks as well as the realization and financing of large-scale projects are guided by a complex set of substantial and procedural

---

[1] COM(94) 860.

legal rules of the Member States and the Union. These are *inter alia* environmental impact assessment, public tender procedures, technical interoperability and standards, company law and tax law, competition rules, the general context of common transport policy, in particular the attribution of infrastructure and external costs, procedures for financial contributions etc. Further important elements lie in the areas of ownership of land and procedures for voluntary or compulsory acquisition with appropriate compensation, as well as in the field of protection of civil rights with the possibility for citizens to defend themselves in the lawcourts if they feel they are affected by a project. The fulfilment of some of these requirements and procedures may cause unpredictable delays and may therefore add to the costs of a project. The fulfilment of other requirements may also do so if not properly planned or managed.

The setting up of public-private partnerships varies from Member State to Member State. The legal systems of Member States provide for different forms and requirements, which are more or less suitable for the purpose. The possibility of giving concessions to private builders and operators, the various forms of introducing equity capital and the fiscal regimes are also relevant factors here, without mentioning the market regimes for all kinds of banking operations.

Where project seminars reveal that a collective approach at the Community level may accelerate procedures, this could be examined at the level of the group.

Energy

In the view of the Commission the realization of the trans-European networks in the energy sector is linked to the realization of the internal market in this area and further market liberalization in the sector of electricity and natural gas. It is recalled that the Commission has taken a position in this area through the enactment of competition rules as well as a number of different proposals.

Although the group has not yet had an opportunity to undertake in-depth analyses of these issues, it is obvious that the physical development of interconnections contributes towards, and is in some cases an important condition for, the effective creation of a more open and competitive energy market, and for reaping the benefits expected from the creation of the internal market generally.

The complexity and, in some cases, slowness of the administrative procedures for obtaining building permissions for energy networks result in many cases in time spans of 5 to 10 years to obtain the necessary authorizations. Environmental considerations are often the central concern in debates on the acceptability of the siting and impact of projects connected with energy networks. Clarification of the rules related to the environmental impact of the projects and of the regulations and standards to be observed could shorten these debates and thereby simplify the authorization procedures.

The Commission's proposals for the Guidelines for trans-European energy networks point out the need for further coordination among Member States in order to tackle difficulties and delays in the implementation of energy networks related to the authorization procedures or the technical aspects applicable to these networks.

Where project seminars reveal that a collective approach at the Community level may accelerate procedures, this could be examined at the level of the group.

General Treaty competition rules

The above considerations on transport and energy should be read bearing in mind the general Treaty provisions as regards competition.

In cases where joint public and private finance is involved, there may be distortion of competition through the use of state aid, (see Article 92) and, in the area of transport, the specific provisions of Articles 77 and 80. The same rules may however allow public financing in cases of projects of Community or public interest, taking into account Title XII of the Treaty and subject to assessment against the established state aids criteria.

Moreover the implications of, *inter alia,* exclusive rights, cooperation between undertakings and agreements between managers and users of networks will have to be addressed in relation to Articles 85 and 90 of the Treaty.

Financing

The Commission has given, in its White Paper and in its recent communication to the Ecofin Council, certain preliminary estimates as regards the total investment needs for TENs over the period to 1999. These figures are indicative. The group has not been in a position to verify these figures sinces in particular, the work of the project seminars is still underway.

The most mature transport projects listed in Appendix 2 represent only a fraction of these totals. However the latest cost estimates for these projects based on data from the Member States broadly confirm the expectations in the White Paper with respect to them. Although cost estimates are uncertain, total investment costs for the eleven projects (excluding the fixed link) are now, on the basis of information collected by the Commission primarily from the Member States, put at over ECU 68 billion in constant prices over their lifetimes (in most cases up to 2002). This amounts to between ECU 4 and 6 billion a year, depending on the phasing of expenditure. The real financial needs in outturn prices will, of course, be higher; the inflation of costs would raise the total financing requirements.

All the figures are being subjected to further review with Member States and other interested parties through the project seminars currently under way.

The group welcomed the paper circulated by the EIB and in particular the suggestions made in it for adapting the terms of the EIB's lending in ways which would take account of the long-term nature of TENs projects.

The group agreed that designation as a trans-European network priority project should not automatically carry with it eligibility for Community finance. To obtain financing from the Community, projects would have to meet the eligibility criteria laid down in the relevant legislation. In particular, finance from the Community budget should not be available for projects which can wholly be financed from the captial markets. Equally, absence from the list does not preclude projects from finance from Community sources.

The group has emphasized that all the priority transport and energy projects must satisfy the test of economic viability. They should be expected to produce a positive net benefit to society, taking into account the external costs and benefits as well as the direct ones. They should as far as possible contribute positively to the competitiveness and the technological development of the Community economy. This requirement, however, does not mean that the projects will necessarily be viable in strict financial or commercial terms, i.e. that their revenues will be sufficient to cover all their costs and produce an adequate return to investors without subsidy. Few of the transport projects are likely to satisfy this test of pure financial viability. Estimated financial rates of return for individual projects range from 3 to 8%, which means that some form of public support will be required, unless external costs and indirect benefits can be internalized.

This financial viability is influenced by the several factors:

☐ A characteristic of many of the transport projects is the long, sometimes uncertain and expensive construction period (6 to 7 years or more is not uncommon) without any revenues to meet financing charges. It is much more difficult for private sector investors to get an early return on their investment than from industrial or commercial projects.

☐ These projects may be affected by a geographical asymmetry between the benefits at Community level and the financial costs associated with the externalities, especially the environmental impact, which occur more regionally or locally.

☐ For transfrontier projects, the need to satisfy different national administrative and legal requirements.

☐ On the revenue side, the single most important factor affecting financial viability is uncertainty about traffic forecasts, both the rate of build-up and the level of traffic flows.

Public/private sector partnerships

The White Paper noted that the major share of the finance needed for TEN investments would be raised at the level of the Member States, either through public budgets, public enterprises or private investors and lenders. Given the nature of the projects in the transport sector, and for the reasons discussed above, the public sector is likely to remain the most important source of finance in transport. In energy and telecommunications, the situation is different. Here the role of the private sector is already established and growing in importance as a result of deregulation, competition and privatization.

Given the constraints on public budgets, which limit the scope for direct financing of investment by the public sector, the rapid realization of the ambitious TEN programmes will, however, demand recourse to different forms of partnership between private and public sectors also in transport. The group, in conformity with the emphasis given by the European Council in Brussels, has stipulated that the priority projects in transport should allow scope for private involvement in a broad sense. Possible forms of involvement are: as a shareholder; as operator of the project under a concession; as a risk-sharing contractor; or as a provider simply of debt finance. One essential requirement is the creation of an appropriate legal and administrative framework for risk-sharing, including where necessary the granting of rights to build, own or operate TEN projects. A second is a closer targeting of public sector support so as specifically to facilitate private sector involvement. Some Member States are already developing approaches such as mini-

mum bids for public budget contributions through tender offers which are intended to minimize the contribution from the public sector and maximize that from the private sector. This targeting must take into account the specific constraints on the supply of private money, taking into consideration that:

☐ most private investors have a shorter time-horizon than the public sector;

☐ the levels of return which they require will be commensurate with risks;

☐ they may be concerned, in the case of physical infrastructure projects, not simply with commercial risk but also 'public policy' risk (changes in legislation or future public investment decisions which affect viability).

Public sector budgets

As far as grant support is concerned, Member States themselves will provide the vast bulk of the necessary funding. For the 10 (excluding Øresund) most mature projects in transport, according to Members States current investment plans, this seems likely to amount to ECU 15 to 20 billion (or between one-quarter and one-third of total investment cost).

TEN projects in eligible regions are also financed by the ERDF and the Cohesion Fund inasmuch as they contribute to the broader objectives of these instruments in the context of economic and social cohesion. The Cohesion Fund (with respect to environment and transport) and the ERDF (in all the TEN sectors), which have significant financial resources at their disposal in the assisted areas of the Union, can finance both grant aids and technical assistance. Some of the priority energy projects, by virtue of their location in and between assisted areas of the Community and their broader impact on regional development, are likely to qualify for ERDF assistance.

The Community also has a specific and complementary role, alongside the Member States, in giving financial support for TEN projects of common interest. It is recalled that the Commission has already proposed a Financial Regulation,[1] based on Article 129 C of the Treaty. This Article allows the Community to support the financial efforts made by the Member States throughout the Union territory for projects of common interest, particularly through feasibility studies, loan guarantees or interest-rate subsidies. The proposal is intended to permit the most effective use of the limitied funds available (on average ECU 400 million a year until 1999) so as to facilitate access by projects of common interest to capital market finance and, where appropriate, to other forms of private sector involvement. It proposes, notably, that promoters should seek the most appropriate lending structure for a project, with the possibility, however, of eligibility for help with interest charges equivalent to up to 10% of the investment cost. It also proposes that the budget could help to meet the costs of underwriting some of the lending arrangements by covering at least a share of the costs of premiums on guarantees. The transport projects, by virtue of their scale and their maturity, are likely to need the greatest recourse to these latter instruments.

Other Community instruments

The largest single source of finance for the TENs at Community level will be the European Investment Bank. In 1993 alone, it lent, through normal lending and its special temporary lending facility ('Edinburgh facility', some ECU 7.5 billion to projects of Community interest in transport, energy and telecommunications as well as ECU 3.5 billion to major environmental projects. Its role in support of the TEN projects

in general and the priorities in particular, will therefore be of particular significance. The group has been able to benefit from the advice of the EIB on the financing aspects. The Commission welcomes the attention which the Bank is giving to this issue and its commitment to making a major additional effort in support of TENs. Specifically, the EIB has identified six areas where additional financial efforts on its part may be useful in some cases, notably with respect to transport projects, namely:

(i) Financing of interest during construction

The EIB already finances interest during construction as part of project costs. It may be possible, with recourse to appropriate funding arrangements, for the Bank also to offer lower rates during construction, recouping the shortfall through capitalization of interest to be repaid over the life of a loan. Such a facility could provide a useful complement to the availability of interest subsidies from the TEN budget-line in reducing the debt service burden in the early stages of projects.

(ii) Extended grace periods for capital repayment

TEN projects also often need to have an extended capital grace period because of the absence of revenues during construction and the slow build-up of positive cash flow after operations begin. The EIB already offers such facilities in some cases and it has in the past provided 'bullet' loans, where capital is repaid in one lump sum at the end of the life of the loan. The Bank is prepared to consider extending this formula more widely to TEN projects.

(iii) Provision of very long maturities

This is a further mechanism intended to minimize the amount of project cash flow which has to be devoted to debt repayment in the early years. The EIB is prepared to provide maturities in excess of 20 years where this is suitable.

---

[1] Ref.: COM(94) 62 final, 2. 3. 1994. Proposal for a Council Regulation laying down general rules for the granting of Community financial aid in the field of trans-European networks.

(iv) Fixing loan rates in advance of drawdown

Advance funding enables project promoters to protect themselves against any increases in interest rates that may occur between the establishment of borrowing facilities and the time that the borrowed funds are needed to finance construction or other costs. The EIB is prepared to establish such facilities where formal commitments have been made to implement the project and where there is a framework agreement between the EIB and the promoter that the funds raised for the promoter's benefit will be duly drawn down.

(v) Cofinancing of project debt

Many banks are prepared to provide construction finance but do not wish to be tied into the project and take revenue risk over a long period. They therefore wish to have arrangements to take them out of the project when it is complete. The EIB is willing to consider structures provided that a framework agreement to this effect has been put in place from the outset as an integral part of the financing arrangements for the project.

(vi) Framework credit agreements

In the case of suitable projects, the EIB will be prepared to enter at an early stage into a framework credit agreement under which it will undertake to provide a substantial part of the finance required, provided that the project promoter meets certain commitments. The amount will obviously vary with circumstances. Disbursements under framework agreements are made through open-rate contracts which give the promoter the possibility, without commitments fees, to draw upon the agreed line of credit at the rate of interest prevailing on capital markets at the time of drawdown (as distinct from the time of initial commitment).

In addition to these specific financing arrangements which should help to attract other sources of finance, the Bank has also offered to play a role in helping to structure the contractual and financing arrangements for priority TEN projects, in collaboration with the promoter and its advisers, the Member States, the Commission and other parties. The EIB's role would be quite specifically to help to devise ways to limit the construction and financing costs and risks of the project.

A further important contribution to facilitating access by these projects to capital market finance should also come from the European Investment Fund, which will be inaugurated in June. The EIF will work with the private sector and with public/private partnerships in helping to allocate and manage risks. The EIF is intended to be a key cofinancing partner with the EIB and other financial institutions in the financing of TENs and SMEs, within the financial ceilings set by its Statute and operating on the basis of proper commercial principles. The EIF should encourage an facilitate various forms of project finance, where debt is backed essentially by cash-flow. This should in time draw institutional investors into these projects. It should also be able to operate closely as a partner with Community budgetary and financial instruments, facilitating their involvement in joint private-public operations. It would be possible, for example, to envisage a TEN financed partly with an EIB loan, partly an EIF guarantee (as on a third party loan), partly with a contribution from the TEN budget line to the EIF premium.

The European Council in December 1993 invited the Ecofin, together with the Commission and the EIB, to study the question of the financing of TENs. The European Council laid emphasis on the objective for the Community of mobilizing larger amounts of private finance for these projects by reducing their financial risks.

Appendices

Appendix 1

List of the personal representatives of the Heads of State or Government

B   Mr. J. Smets
    Chef de Cabinet du Premier Ministre pour la Cellule économique et sociale

D   Mr. G. Haller
    Staatssekretär im Bundesministerium für Finanzen

DK Mr. J. Thomsen
    Departementchef i Oekonomiministeriet

GR Mr. L. Nikolaou
    Permanent Adviser to the Prime Minister

E   Mr. J. A. Zaragoza
    Secretario de Estado de Politica Territorial y Obras Publicas

F   Mr. P. de Boissieu
    Représentant Permanent de la France auprès de l'Union Européénne

IRL Mr. J. Loughrey
    The Secretary, Department of Transport, Energy and Communications

I   Mr. A. Minuto Rizzo
    Consigliere diplomatico del Ministro del bilancio e della programmazione
    economica

L   Mr. G. Reinesch
    Commissaire du Gouvernement

NL Mr. T. Van de Graaf
    Raadadviseur voor Financiële economische aangelegenheden en voor infra-
    structuur
    Waarnemend Secretaris-Generaal van het Ministerie van Algemene Zaken

P   Mr. J. Peneda
    Deputato da Assembleia da Republica

UK Mr. G. Fitchew
    Head of European Secretariat of the Cabinet Office

* * *

Sir Brian Unwin, President of the EIB, also took part in the work of the group.

Appendix 2

List of transport priority projects

I. Work already begun or to begin within 2 years

1. *High-speed train/combined transport north-south*   I/A/D
   Brenner axis Verona — Munich — Nuremberg — Erfurt
   — Halle/Leipzig — Berlin

2. *High-speed train (Paris —) Brussels — Cologne — Amsterdam — London*
   The following sections of the project are included

   Belgium: F/B border — Brussels — Liège — B/D border;   B
   Brussels — B/NL border
   United Kingdom: London — Channel Tunnel access   UK
   Netherlands: B/NL border — Rotterdam — Amsterdam   NL
   Germany: (Aachen —) [1] Cologne — Rhine/Main   D

3. *High-speed train south*
   Madrid — Barcelona — Perpignan   E/(F)
   Madrid — Vitoria — Dax   E/(F)

4. *High-speed train east*
   The following sections of the project are included [2]

   Paris — Metz — Strasbourg — Appenweier
   (— Karlsruhe)   F/D
   with junctions to Metz — Saarbrücken — Mannheim   F/D
   and Metz — Luxembourg   F/L

5. *Betuwe line: Combined transport/conventional rail*   NL/D
   Rotterdam — NL/D border (— Rhine/Ruhr) [1]

6. *High-speed train/combined transport France — Italy*
   Lyons — Turin   F/I

7. *Motorway Patras — Greek/Bulgarian border/*   GR
   together with the West-East motorway corridor:
   Via Egnatia
   Igoumenitsa — Thessaloniki — Alexandroupolis

8. *Motorway Lisbon — Valladolid*   P/E

9. *Cork — Dublin — Belfast — Larne — Stranraer rail link*   IRL/UK

---

[1] Ongoing construction support already provided at Community level.

[2] The extension to Frankfurt is already under construction; as regards the further extension to Berlin the maturity of the project is
not advanced enough.

10.	*Malpensa airport (Milan)*	I
11.	*Fixed rail/road link between Denmark and Sweden (Øresund fixed link)* [1] including Danish access routes	DK/S

II. Acceleration possible so that work can begin in about 2 years

12.	*Combined transport* up to now projects identified in France, Germany, Italy, Belgium, Portugal and Spain	EU-wide
13.	*Motorway Nuremberg — Prague*	D/(Cz)
14.	*Motorway Berlin — Warsaw (— Moscow)* in parallel with: High-speed train link Berlin — Warsaw (— Moscow)	D/(Pol)
15.	*Motorway Dresden — Prague*	D/(Cz)
16.	*Ireland/United Kingdom/Benelux road link*	UK/(IRL)
17.	*Spata airport*	GR
18.	*Berlin airport*	D
19.	*Autoroute de la Maurienne*	F
20.	*Autoroute Marateca — Elvas*	P
21.	*High-speed train in Denmark*	DK

III. Projects which need to be examined further

22.	*Fehmarn Belt: fixed link between Denmark and Germany*	DK/D
23.	*Motorway Bari — Otranto*	I
24.	*Canal Rhine — Rhone*	F
25.	*Canal Seine — Schelde*	F
26.	*Canal Elbe — Oder*	D
27.	*Danube upgrading between Straubing and Vilshofen*	D
28.	*High-speed train Randstad — Rhine/Ruhr Amsterdam — Arnhem (— Cologne)*	NL
29.	*Road corridor Valencia — Zaragoza — Somport*	E
30.	*High-speed train Turin — Venice — Trieste*	I
31.	*High-speed train (Brenner —) Milan — Rome — Naples*	I
32.	*Trans Apennine highway Bologna — Florence*	I
33.	*Magnetic levitation train: Transrapid*	D
34.	*High-speed train connection Luxembourg — Brussels*	B/L

---

[1] Subject to approval by the Swedish government.

Europe-wide projects

With regard to the projects which deal with the implementation of new technologies on a European-wide basis, i.e. those which relate to traffic management and which will improve the use of infrastructure for all modes of transport (land, sea, air), the Commission will submit the appropriate proposals on how to proceed as soon as possible with the following projects;

☐ road traffic management system,
☐ air traffic management system,
☐ vessel traffic management system,
☐ multimodal positioning system by satellites,
☐ pilot projects for a railway management system.

Appendix 3

Description of the transport priority projects

In part A of this appendix an overview is provided on the state of the trans-European transport network's development.

Part B of this appendix deals with the most mature priority projects under examination in the group.

Part C concerns the extension of the networks to the Central and East European countries, drawing together the main elements of the second Pan-European Transport Conference held in Crete in March this year.

A. Trans-European transport network

The Commission adopted a proposal for a Council and European Parliament decision on Community guidelines for the development of a trans-European network on 29 March 1994 (COM(94) 106). To summarize the work done so far at Community level, network outline plans for roads, high-speed railways, combined transport and inland waterways are included on the following pages.

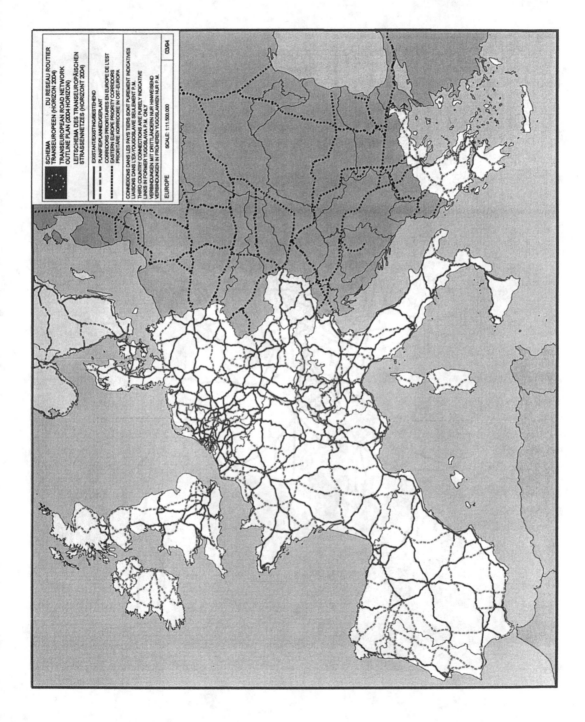

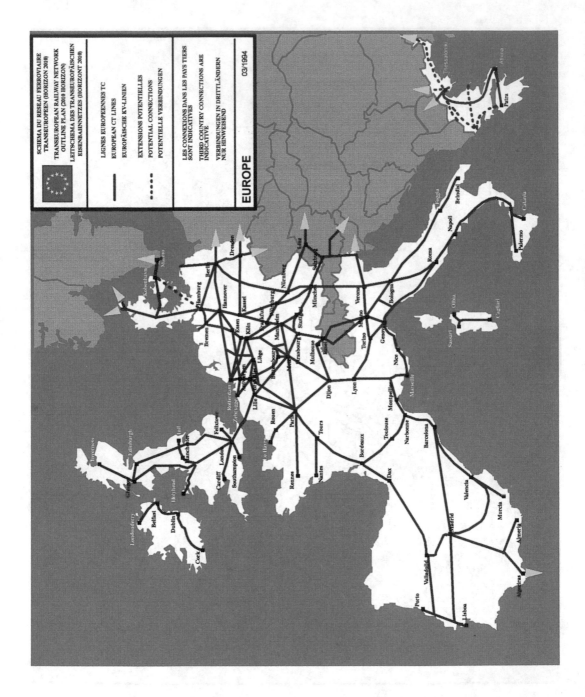

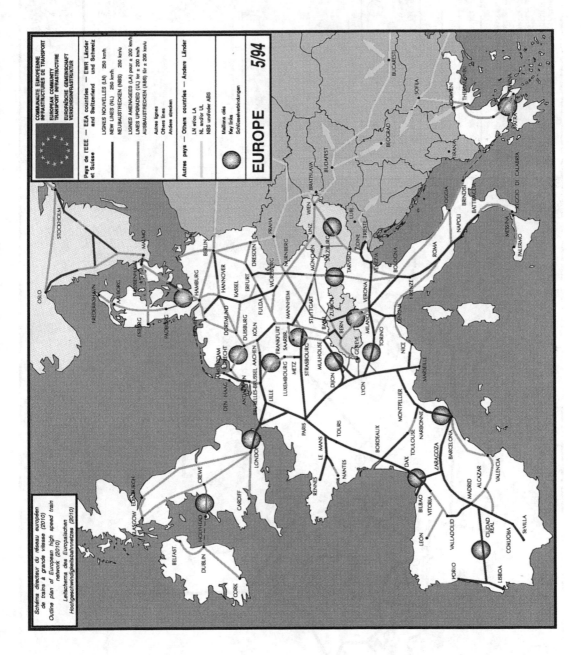

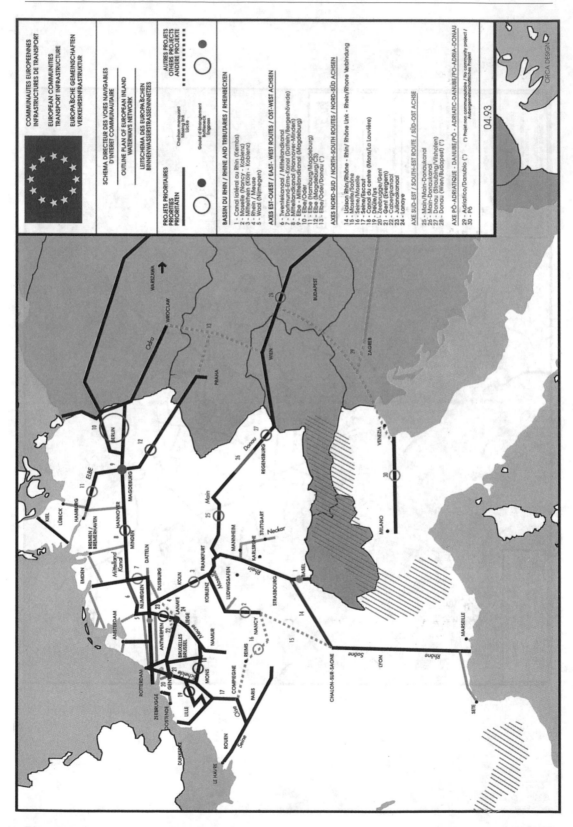

B. Description of the most mature transport priority projects

Based on a set of criteria outlined in the main paper the Christophersen group has identified 11 projects which are of priority as far as the completion of the integrated trans-European transport network is concerned (guidelines proposed by the Commission and submitted to the Council, the European Parliament, the Economic and Social Committee and the Committee of Regions in April 1994). The starting point for this was the indicative list of 26 transport projects included in the White Paper and further Member States' proposals regarding this list. These projects show a high degree of maturity. Their realization has either already been started or is expected to begin within the next two years.

Distinguishing characteristics of the 11 projects are, first of all, their large scale (total investment of about ECU 68.5 billion, excluding the Øresund fixed link) and secondly their great significance as far as the connection of national transport networks is concerned. Eight of them involve from two to five Member States, three are crucial as regards linking islands (Ireland/Northern Ireland) and peripheral countries (Greece, Portugal) with the central areas of the Union. One project plays an important role with respect to exchanges between the Union and the rest of the world, namely Malpensa airport.

The composition of this group of projects shows that, in planning transport infrastructure projects, much attention has been paid to the aspect of environmental protection. In all 88% of the total investment will be dedicated to railways, which will have a positive impact both on passenger and freight traffic: by decisively reducing the travelling time between a number of European capitals (ie the high-speed trains Paris — Brussels — Cologne — Amsterdam — London and the Paris — eastern France — southern Germany projects), the attractiveness of this mode will be increased and some passenger traffic will be encouraged to switch from road or short-haul flights to the more environmentally friendly rail; projects such as the Brenner axis and the Lyons — Turin link, which entail both capacity and quality increases for freight traffic and give further impetus to the development of combined transport, will also have a positive impact on the environment and not least the economy.

Whereas these most mature transport projects form, on the one hand, strategic links which contribute to the economic growth and competitiveness of the Union as a whole, they have, on the other hand, a decisive impact on prosperity in the regions directly concerned; the completion of the 11 projects will lead to the creation of a noticeable number of permanent jobs.

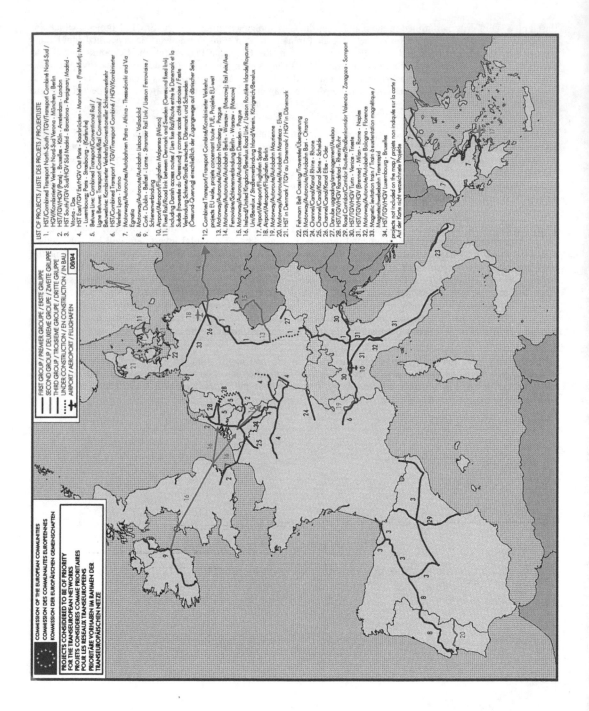

High-speed train/combined transport north — south including Brenner axis

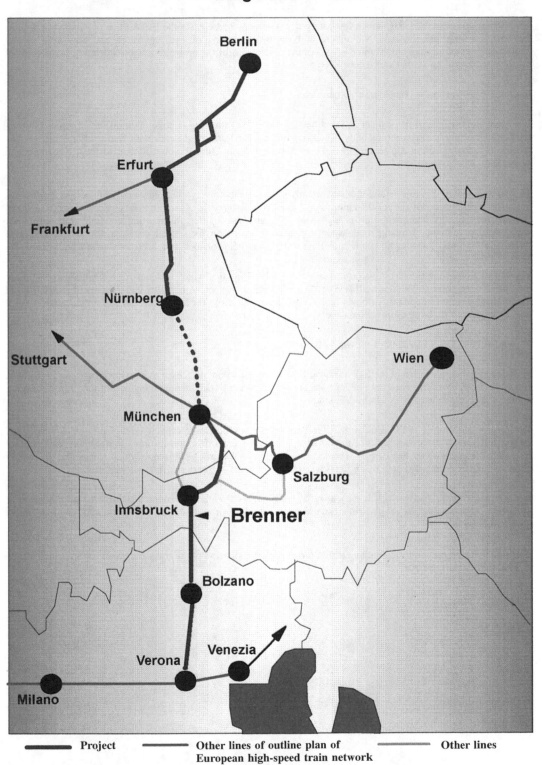

Legend:

Project	Other lines of outline plan of European high-speed train network	Other lines

This project represents an important part of the European north — south high-speed rail/combined transport corridor Berlin — Munich — Roma/Adria — Greece and is part of the trans-European transport network. It contributes to providing access to potential Member States. The project comprises two sections.

The 409 km long Brenner axis, which links Italy with Germany and crosses the EFTA State of Austria, as well as the 550 km long link between Nuremberg and Berlin (upgrading of existing tracks and new construction respectively). The missing link Munich — Nuremberg is not part of the project but is considered to be of national priority; work will be started very soon.

Brenner Axis Verona — Innsbruck — Munich

The great significance of this project is, in particular, due to the following factors: the transport of goods between Italy and Germany has been permanently increasing; on Austrian territory, the enormous traffic volume has to cross the ecologically sensitive Alpine region and the existing infrastructure is not sufficient to meet environmental considerations.

The heavy goods traffic uses, at the moment, mainly the Alpine motorway; this causes not only severe burdens for the inhabitants concerned and for the environment but also considerable economic losses since the traffic demand exceeds the capacity and congestion is increasing. The alternative offer, transporting goods by rail, is not yet sufficiently developed. A rolling road, which has been in operation for several years, is not attractive enough (relatively low speed, waiting time at terminals) and thus does not contribute to a decisive switch from road to rail.

The completion of the Brenner-Axis project, a high-speed railway line which includes the construction of a 55 km long base tunnel through the Alps, will lead to a considerable improvement in quality and capacity of rail traffic and by doing so have an important ecological and economic impact. Both for freight and for passenger traffic, choice will be improved (halving of travelling time).

Nuremberg — Erfurt — Halle/Leipzig — Berlin

Included in the continuation of the link northwards is the construction of 250 km of new track between Lichtenfels and Halle/Leipzig, so that speed can be increased to up to 250 km/h. On the remaining part of the project, existing tracks will be upgraded for speeds of 200 km/h.

The project contributes, in the same way as the Brenner axis, to increasing capacity and quality of passenger and freight traffic and represents another important element of the north-south corridor. Furthermore in Erfurt, it intersects the east — west link Paris — Frankfurt — Berlin — (Warsaw — Moscow) which means that the section Erfurt — Berlin forms part both of an important European north — south and east — west link.

In the new German *Länder,* which at present suffer considerably from an economic downturn, the improvement of transport infrastructure is of particular significance in view of stimulating investors and creating direct project-related jobs.

The realization of the project is fundamental to the envisaged extension of the trans-European transport network to Central and Eastern Europe.

High-speed train Paris — Brussels — Cologne — Amsterdam — London (PBKAL)

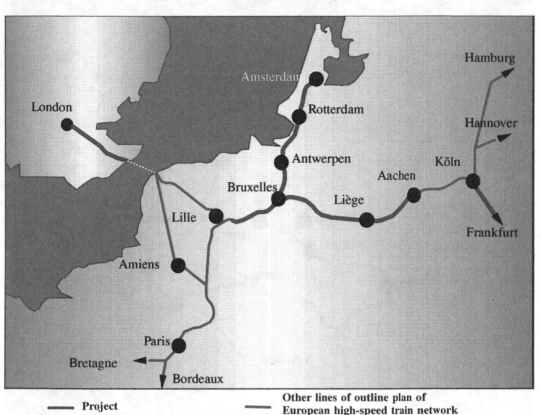

——— **Project**

━━━ **Other lines of outline plan of European high-speed train network**

One of the most important projects of the Union's transport infrastructure programme is the PBKAL project (total investment: ECU 12.9 billion). As regards the trans-European high-speed railway network (Council Resolution of 17 December 1990), it is the first project upon which the governments concerned have concluded an agreement as to its construction.

The PBKAL project consists of the following sections:

☐ Channel tunnel access — Lille — Paris/Brussels
☐ Brussels — Cologne
☐ Brussels — Amsterdam
☐ Channel tunnel access — London.

Noticeable reductions in travelling time between European capitals and other important cities can be expected as soon as the project is completed, e.g. Brussels — London: 4 hours 55 minutes reduced to 2 hours 05 minutes; Brussels — Paris: 2 hours 25 minutes reduced to 1 hour 20 minutes; Brussels — Amsterdam: 2 hours 45 minutes reduced to 1 hour 30 minutes; Brussels — Frankfurt: 5 hours 20 minutes reduced to 2 hours 55 minutes. It establishes thus an interesting alternative to inner-EU short-haul flights.

By creating new, high quality links for passenger traffic, the existing conventional railway network will be relieved. This will contribute to improved conditions for freight traffic using the conventional network. The creation of the new links will lead to an increase in rail capacity and a reduction of irregularities. This will make rail transport more attractive and help further to stimulate the switch from rail to road, in particular for long and medium-distance journeys — to the benefit of the environment.

With the entry into operation of the Paris — Lille section and, in particular, of the Channel Tunnel, the first steps in the completion of this large scale European project, connecting important political, commercial and cultural centres, have been taken.

High-speed train south

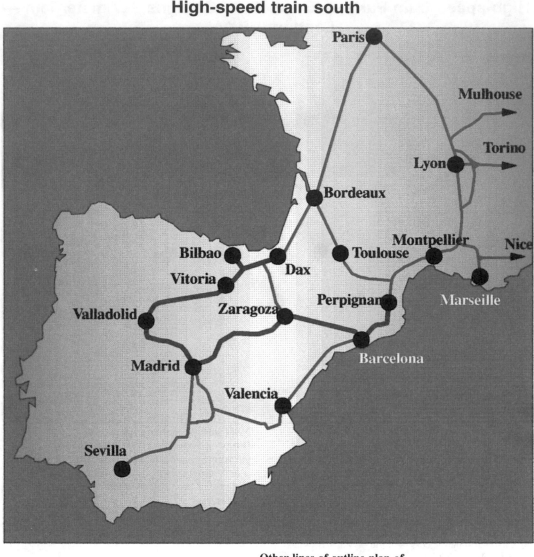

━━━ Project

━━━ Other lines of outline plan of European high-speed train network

This project consists of two links between the Iberian Peninsula and the French high-speed train network. In its Mediterranean side, it goes from Madrid to Perpignan via Zaragoza and Barcelona. Its Atlantic part makes the connection with the French 'TGV Atlantique' possible (via Valladolid and Vitoria).

The length of the future high-speed railway line amounts to 1 450 km, 1 200 km of which represent the construction of new tracks. Between Valladolid and Vitoria, existing tracks will be upgraded so that speeds of up to 200 km/h can be reached. A particularly difficult section of the new line is the Pyrenees crossing (of the 170 km of new tracks, 40% will go through tunnels).

The most significant benefit of the completion of this project is the extension of European standard gauge to the Spanish network. This reduces track/vehicle related stops at the border crossings, thus contributing to solving interoperability problems.

Both the Atlantic and the Mediterranean parts of the new high-speed railway line will be used for passenger and freight traffic. The realization of the links will lead to noticeable capacity increases (i.e. Madrid — Barcelona by 400%) and reductions in travelling time (i.e. Madrid — Barcelona by 4 hours). The project is therefore of great importance in view of the improvement of commercial relations between Spain and the central part of the Union, and has a positive impact on the economic development in the regions concerned.

High-speed train east Paris — eastern France — southern Germany

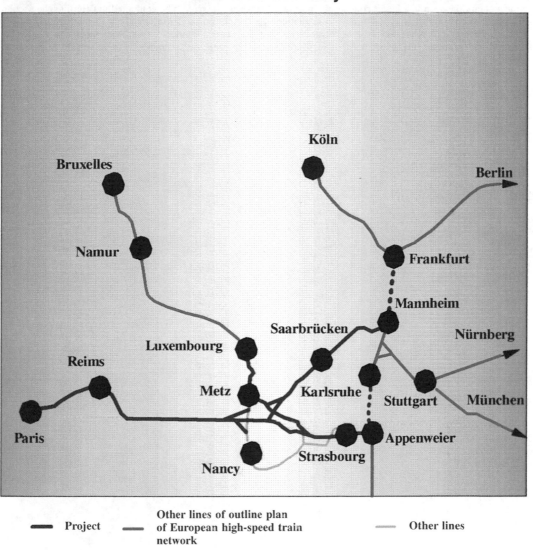

| | Project | | Other lines of outline plan of European high-speed train network | | Other lines |

With the introduction of the Paris — eastern France — southern Germany project an important European east — west axis will be completed. It will be of great significance, not only for the connection of such important centres as Paris and Frankfurt (seat of the future European Central Bank) but also for connections between the European institutions as well as with Central and Eastern Europe. In 1992, the French and the German governments concluded an agreement on the implementation of this project.

Included in the project is the construction of a new line from Paris to the eastern border of France where, at two points, the French and German high-speed railway networks are linked with each other (Forbach/Saarbrücken and Strasbourg/Kehl). Furthermore a branch will be constructed which links Metz with Luxembourg. (It is also to be noted that in the context of sub-group III the modernization of the Brussels — Luxembourg line is under study.)

Connecting French and German networks would allow noticeable reductions in travelling time for such important connections as Paris — Munich (8 hours 40 minutes compared to 4 hours 25 minutes) and Paris — Frankfurt (5 hours 55 minutes compared to 3 hours 10 minutes).

In the French part of the project 460 km of new line is to be constructed. The German part includes the two branches F/D border — Saarbrücken — Ludwigshafen/Mannheim (128 km to be upgraded for speeds of up to 200 km/h) and (Strasbourg) — F/D border — Kehl — Appenweier (17 km to be upgraded for speeds of up to 200 km/h). The project should be seen in a larger context: the northern branch is foreseen to be continued via Berlin. The section Mannheim — Frankfurt is already under construction. The extension to Berlin is subject to the national master scheme, further studies are however necessary. The southern branch continues from Appenweier to Karlsruhe, Stuttgart and Munich. Besides the east — west connection the project also envisages an extension to the south (Basle).

Betuwe line

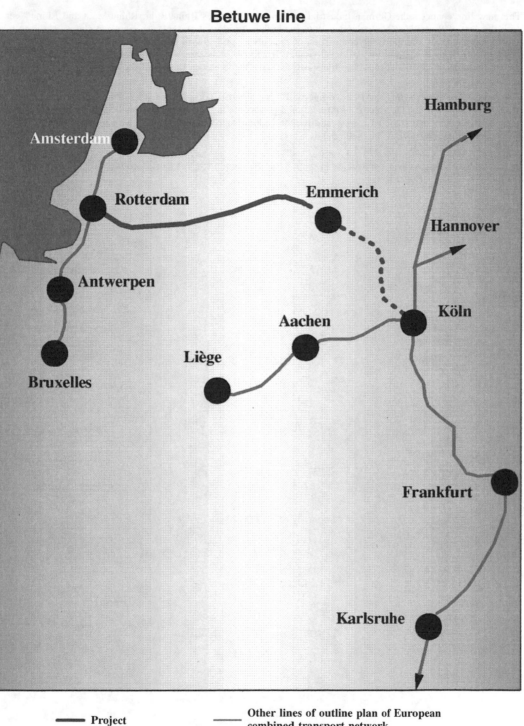

— **Project**

—— **Other lines of outline plan of European combined transport network**

■■■■ **In construction**

The Betuwe line project consists of the construction of a new 160 km long conventional railway line. It will directly improve the capacity of goods transport and will increase indirectly the capacity for passenger traffic on the existing network in a densely populated area in the northern part of Europe.

This new line connects the German industrial and consumer centres Rhine/Ruhr, Rhine/Main and Rhine/Neckar with the port of Rotterdam (Netherlands). Whereas in this corridor, at present, the users can choose between road and inland waterway transport, the completion of the railway project will bring about a third land transport mode and so contributes to the multimodal development. It will facilitate the switch to more environmentally friendly transport chains, e.g. rail and maritime transport, and take heavy goods traffic off the roads.

The increase in capacity that the Betuwe line will bring about is considerable (capacity: 150 million tonnes per year). It is estimated that the volume of international goods entering the Netherlands will increase by 50% until the year 2010. In this context the east — west direction is dominant, and the new Betuwe Line will account for half of the rail freight capacity of the Netherlands.

In addition, the Betuwe line contributes to completing the combined transport corridor Italy — Switzerland — Germany — Port of Rotterdam.

High-speed train/combined transport Lyons — Turin

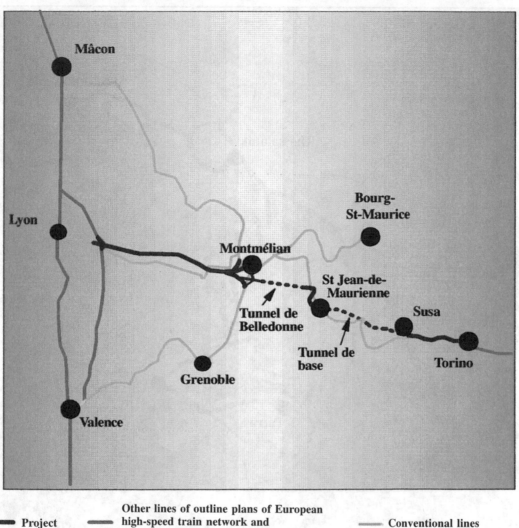

Project ── **Other lines of outline plans of European high-speed train network and combined transport network** ── **Conventional lines**

The project is of great European importance since it improves substantially the Alpine crossing rail connection from France to Italy. This line continues in Italy via Milano both to the centre and Greece on the one side, and to Austria and Slovenia on the other. In Lyons two important corridors join the line: the first to and from the UK — Paris and the second to and from the Iberian Peninsula.

The Lyons — Turin project includes respectively the construction and upgrading of lines of a total length of 250 km. The section through the Alps requires particular technical and financial efforts — a 54 km long base tunnel has to be constructed. The benefits to passenger traffic will be substantial: the travelling time between Barcelona and Milan, after completion of the project, will be 5 hours 25 minutes compared with 12 hours 45 minutes at present.

Because of the high construction cost, the section of the new line between Montmelian and Turin will be used for both passenger and freight traffic. The line belongs to the trans-European combined transport network, and its completion increases the capacity for freight traffic considerably which in turn facilitates commercial exchanges in a wider European context in an environmentally friendly way.

It should be noted that the regions covered by the project, Rhone-Alps, Piedmont and Lombardy, are among the most prosperous in the Union and thus have a real need to improve their transport communications.

Motorways PATHE and via Egnatia

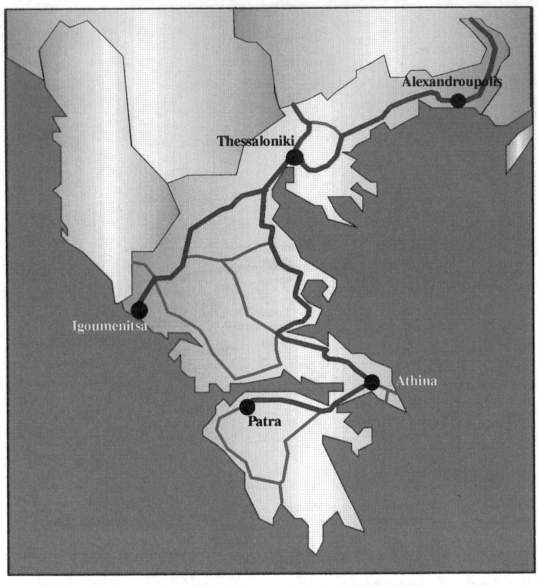

—— **Project**   **——** **Other roads of outline plan
of European road network**

The project which will be a backbone for the Greek motorway system is crucial to the transport infrastructure development in Greece. It connects (via branches) the isolated Union member state with all of its neighbours: Albania, Bulgaria, FYROM and Turkey. Via the connection to sea ports, it makes relations with Italy possible (i.e. rolling road Igoumenitsa — Italian ports). The following two sections form the project:

☐ the Patras — Athens — Thessaloniki — Greek/Bulgarian border motorway (PATHE)

☐ the Igoumenitsa — Thessaloniki — Alexandroupolis motorway (via Egnatia).

Both sections represent projects of exceptional scale: the new PATHE motorway will be 860 km long; 200 km have already been completed, 100 km are at present under construction. The axis connects the most important Greek cities; it belongs to a corridor which crosses several southern European countries and goes to Germany.

The via Egnatia project involves the construction of 780 km of new motorway; the axis traverses northern Greece, from the port of Igoumenitsa on the west cost of Ionian sea to Kipi (at the Greek/Turkish border) and Ormenio (at the Greek/Bulgarian border) on the east side of the country. Via RoRo, it will be connected to the Italian motorway system. It is planned as a dual two-lane motorway; on the Igoumenitsa — Thessaloniki mountainous section only, for long tunnels and large bridges, initially, one carriageway will be implemented to reduce cost.

Along both axes, about 70% of the Greek population is distributed. The realization of the projects will therefore have a positive impact on the economic development.

Motorway Lisbon — Valladolid

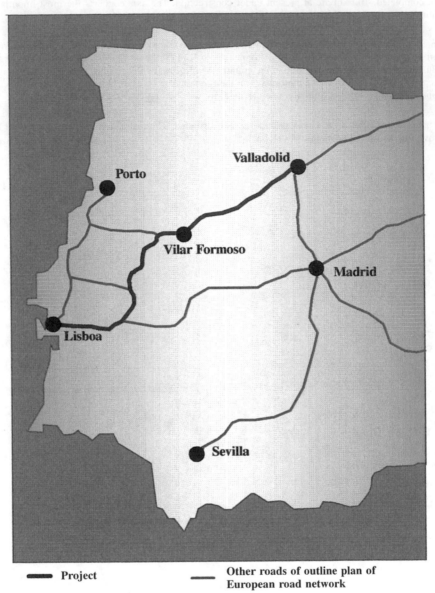

▬▬ Project **▬▬ Other roads of outline plan of European road network**

This project is of great significance in other to link the Portuguese motorway network with the Spanish and French networks. In the regions directly concerned, it will stimulate economic and regional development and by doing so, it contributes to social and economic cohesion within the European Union.

The Lisbon — Valladolid motorway project includes the upgrading and partial realignment of an existing road to motorway standard. The total length of the axis amounts to 460 km. With the completion of the project, a direct and uncongested link between Lisbon — northern Spain and France will be provided and the traffic flow on the alternative road network will be facilitated. The reduction in traffic congestion will bring about positive environmental effects; by improving traffic safety the social costs will be reduced.

Both Portugal and Spain are among the countries which have already gained some experience as regards concessions for motorways. Users could be prepared to pay charges, which will certainly encourage the involvement of the private sector.

Conventional rail/combined transport
Cork — Dublin — Belfast — Larne — Stranraer

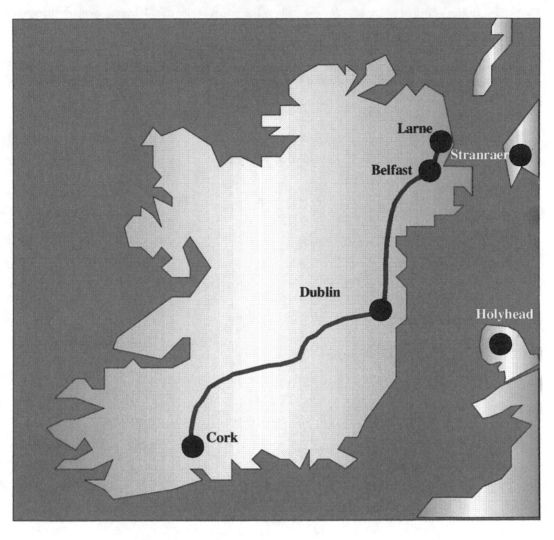

— Project

This project complements the 'T-shaped' trans-European north-south rail link Cork — Dublin — Belfast — Larne (ferry links Ireland — Great Britain) — Holyhead — London — Channel Tunnel/Benelux countries. The Cork — Dublin — Belfast — Larne rail axis is the key central spine of the Irish railway network. It is the only cross-border line in the network, provides a crucial transport link between Northern Ireland and Ireland and is vital to the connection with the British network.

The Irish plans for the link include a gradual upgrading of the existing line for a maximum speed of 175 km/h between Cork and Dublin and 145 km/h between Dublin and Belfast. The total length of the project amounts to about 520 km. The line is intended to serve both passenger and freight traffic. Several ferry lines provide the connections, for passenger and freight traffic, with the British rail network.

The completion of the project will establish an interesting alternative to road and air traffic and by doing so contribute to a more environmentally friendly transport system and improve the modal choice.

The Cork — Dublin — Belfast — Larne — Stranraer railway line belongs to the trans-European combined transport network which underlines the objective of encouraging the switch from road to rail in the freight transport sector, especially as far as long distance journeys are concerned.

As regards the further economic development of Ireland, the project plays an important role. Not only during construction but also once the line is completed it will have a noticeable positive effect on the labour market.

Malpensa airport

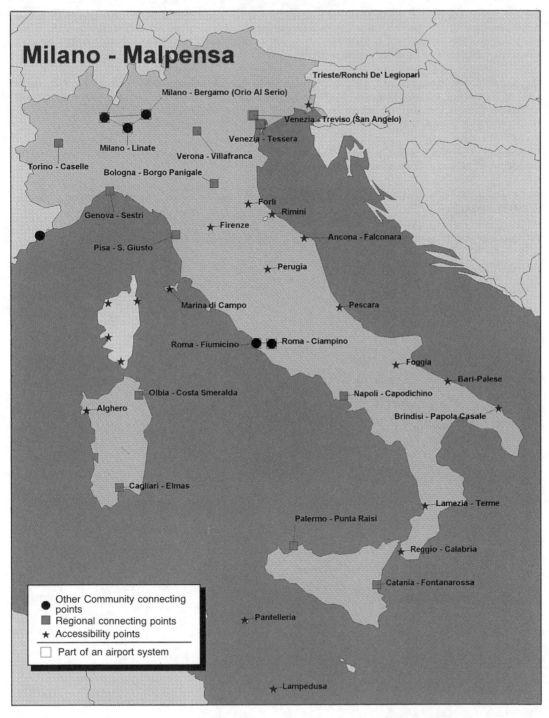

Malpensa airport is part of the Milan airport system, located in the northern part of Italy. The existing Malpensa airport is being modernized and extended so that it will become the hub for northern Italy and thus the most significant element of the airport system. The planned rail link between this airport and the city centre will allow for relatively short journey times. Short-haul flights will continue to be operated from Linate airport which is located closer to the city centre.

The development of the airport will enable the concentration of intercontinental and EU flights in a single airport in northern Italy. It will, thus, contribute to connecting an important commercial and cultural centre of the Union with the rest of the world. The new Malpensa airport will facilitate exchanges between Europe and its partners, which is a vital factor for future economic progress.

The project is entirely in line with the objectives related to the development of the trans-European transport network: it allows for the interconnection of land (high-speed train, conventional rail, combined transport, road) and air transport modes and, thus, the achievement of highly efficient transport chains for passengers and freight. Malpensa airport is planned to become an important European intermodal terminal.

The location of Malpensa airport, at about 50 km from the city centre, will make it possible better to contain the environmental impact in terms of noise pollution.

The new Malpensa airport will directly create 6 000 permanent jobs; the indirect impact is estimated at another 12 000 to 18 000 jobs.

This demonstrates the great importance of the project for the development of northern Italy.

Fixed rail/road link between Denmark and Sweden (Øresund) including Danish access route

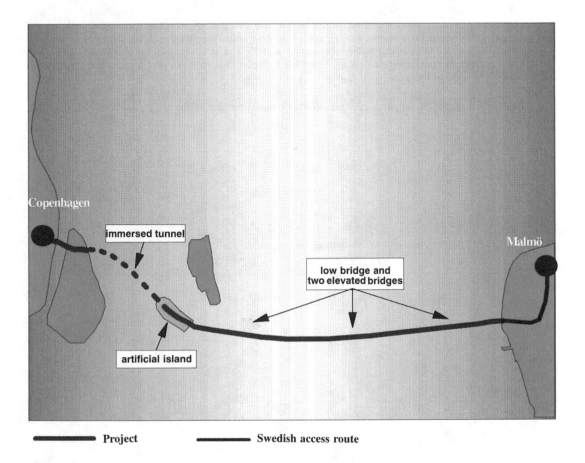

Copenhagen

immersed tunnel

low bridge and two elevated bridges

artificial island

Malmö

━━━━━ Project   ━━━━━ Swedish access route

The construction of the first fixed link between Denmark and the potential EU Member State Sweden will create the basis for a considerably improved flow of traffic, especially by train, between these two countries. It will thus contribute towards meeting increasing demands within the freight and passenger sectors as a result of the forthcoming extension of the Union, as regards both quality and capacity.

The project can be divided into two parts: the rail and road access between Copenhagen and the coast, and the Øresund fixed link. It forms not only an important part of the Copenhagen — Malmö link but also an important link between Scandinavia and the continent.

In 1991 the Danish and the Swedish Parliaments had agreed on the realization of this project; its completion foreseen for the year 2000. After entry into operation the new link will lead to a marked reduction in travelling time, when compared with the present crossing by ferry (e.g. 1 hour for cars). In addition, it will provide an important capacity increase; in particular the passenger traffic by rail is expected to increase substantially (by 450%).

The two parts of the project have the following characteristics:

☐ *Access on the Danish land side:*
four-lane motorway, 10 km in length,
double-track railway, 12 km in length with approximately 5 km of shunt railway.

☐ *Fixed link over the Øresund*

The fixed link, including double-track railway line and a four-lane motorway, will be approximately 16 km long. It is subdivided into three parts: a 3.8 km long tunnel (near the Danish coast), a 4.2 km long artificial island and a 7.5 km long bridge of which 1.1 km is elevated and 6.4 km is low-level.

According to the agreement between the Danish and the Swedish governments, the fixed link will be built, owned and operated by a bi-national consortium, with both States as share holders (collection of user charges for the road). Construction work on the Danish access route was started in 1993. The Swedish government has not yet finalized the decision procedures concerning the project. A decision is expected to be made very soon so that construction work can start by 1995 at the latest.

The total employment for the project is estimated to 42 000 man-years during the design and construction period.

C. The extension of trans-European networks to Eastern Europe

Three years after the first Pan-European Transport Conference in Prague in October 1991 a second Conference took place in Crete in March 1994 to reflect the developments so far and to establish a basis for future work. The approach is outlined below.

The Commission has worked on an informal basis with the European Conference of Ministers of Transport (ECMT), the United Nations Economic Commission for Europe (UN/ECE), the countries of Central and Eastern Europe and EFTA and the Member States of the European Union as well as the World Bank, the European Bank for Reconstruction and Development and the European Investment Bank with a view to preparing Indicative Guidelines for the further development of the pan-European transport infrastructure. These would serve the purpose of promoting interconnection and interoperability of networks in Europe by focusing attention on priority transport infrastructure projets of common interest, including maintenance, rehabilitation and border crossing facilitation, thus contributing to the gradual integration of the European continent.

The approach is based on a concept of three layers and has been considered by the Conference as a starting point. The three layers (the second layer is reflected on the attached map) consist of:

Layer 1:   The long term perspective for pan-European development of common interest on the basis of the United Nations conventions on European infrastructure planning for road, rail and combined transport (AGR, AGC, AGTC). No time horizon.

Layer 2:   The priorities of common interest for medium-term development (2010). TENs for the Union territory and priority multimodal corridors towards central and eastern European countries (see attached maps).

Layer 3:   The short term priority projects of kommon interest located on layer 2, expected to be implemented within 5 years, to be selected on basis of agreed operational criteria (only Central and Eastern Europe).

Based on the above mentioned operational criteria and proposals put forward by Member States directly concerned the following projects will be looked at more closely:

☐ Berlin — Moscow (road and rail)
☐ Nuremberg — Prague
☐ Dresden — Prague
☐ Hungary Highway M5
☐ Danube fixed crossing (road and rail).

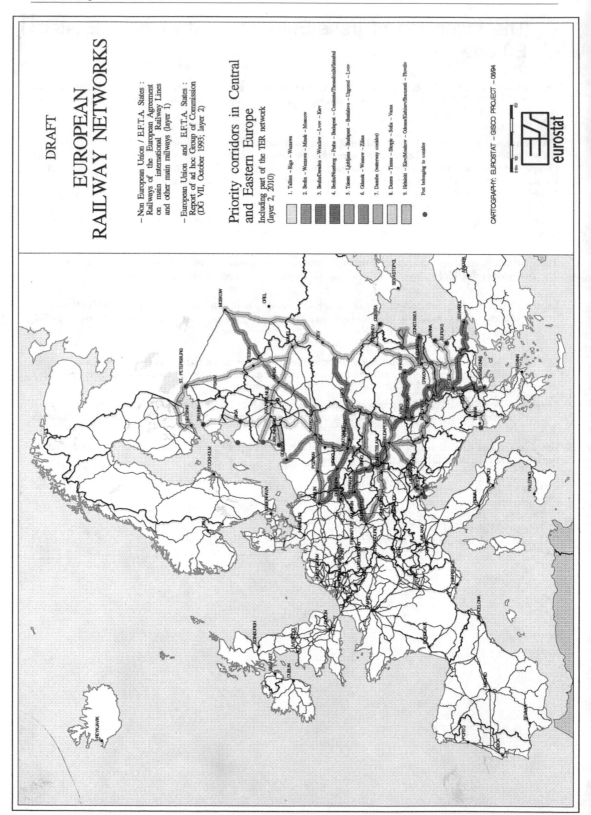

DRAFT

EUROPEAN RAILWAY NETWORKS

- Non European Union / E.F.T.A. States :
  Railways of the European Agreement
  on main international Railway Lines
  and other main railways (layer 1)

- European Union and E.F.T.A. States :
  Report of ad hoc Group of Commission
  (DG VII; October 1993; layer 2)

Priority corridors in Central and Eastern Europe

Including part of the TER network
(layer 2, 2010)

1. Tallinn – Riga – Warsaw
2. Berlin – Warsaw – Minsk – Moscow
3. Berlin/Dresden – Wroclaw – Lvov – Kiev
4. Berlin/Nurnberg – Praha – Budapest – Constanta/Thessaloniki/Istanbul
5. Trieste – Ljubljana – Budapest – Bratislava – Uzgorod –Lvov
6. Gdansk – Warsaw – Zilina
7. Danube (waterway corridor)
8. Durres – Tirana – Skopje – Sofia – Varna
9. Helsinki – Kiev/Moscow – Odessa/Kishinev/Bucuresti – Plovdiv

● Port belonging to corridor

CARTOGRAPHY: EUROSTAT – GISCO PROJECT – 0694

eurostat

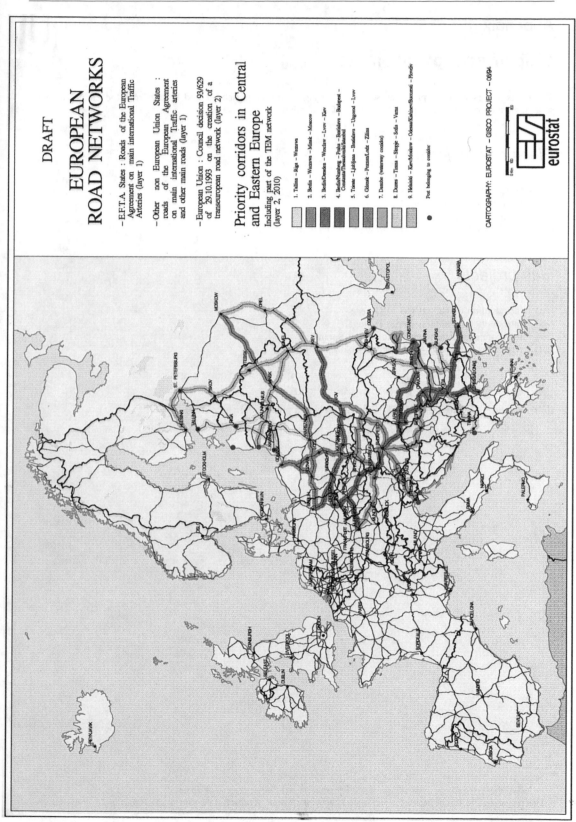

DRAFT

EUROPEAN ROAD NETWORKS

– E.F.T.A. States : Roads of the European Agreement on main international Traffic Arteries (layer 1)

– Other non European Union States : roads of the European Agreement on main international Traffic arteries and other main roads (layer 1)

– European Union : Council decision 93/629 of 29.10.1993 on the creation of a transeuropean road network (layer 2)

Priority corridors in Central and Eastern Europe
Including part of the TEM network (layer 2, 2010)

1. Tallinn – Riga – Warzawa
2. Berlin – Warzawa – Minsk – Moscow
3. Berlin/Dresden – Wroclaw – Lvov – Kiev
4. Berlin/Nurnberg – Praha – Bratislava – Budapest – Constanta/Thessaloniki/Istanbul
5. Trieste – Ljubljana – Bratislava – Uzgorod – Lvov
6. Gdansk – Poznan/Lodz – Zilina
7. Danube (waterway corridor)
8. Durres – Tirana – Skopje – Sofia – Varna
9. Helsinki – Kiev/Moskow – Odessa/Kishinev/Bucuresti – Plovdiv

● Port belonging to consider

CARTOGRAPHY: EUROSTAT - GISCO PROJECT - 06/94

eurostat

Appendix 4

List of energy projects

The Christophersen group proposes selecting the eight priority projects listed below from the energy network schemes which could be completed in the short or medium-term:

Electricity projects [1]

(a4)   Greece-Italy interconnection (cable)
(b6)   France-Italy interconnection
(b10) Spain-Portugal interconnection
(c2)   Cable link between eastern and western Denmark

Gas projects [1]

(e6)   Introduction of natural gas in Greece
(e5)   Introduction of natural gas in Portugal
(f6)   Interconnection between Portugal and Spain [2]
(h4)   Algeria — Morocco — European Union pipeline

* * *

(h7)   Russia — Belarus — Poland — European Union pipeline [3]

---

[1] Same project codes as in the guidelines proposal [COM(93) 685].
[2] Including the introduction of natural gas in the Extremadura and Galicia regions of Spain.
[3] This project should also be shortlisted and studied although it has not yet reached the same stage as the other four gas schemes.

Appendix 5

Description of the energy projects

Electricity projects

Underground electricity cable to interconnect Italy and Greece (a4)

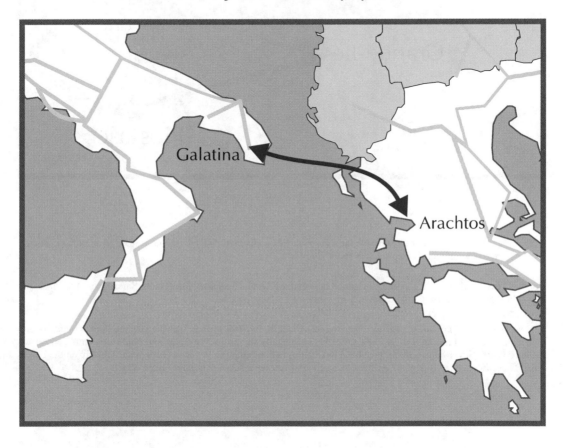

This project is of great strategic importance since it will provide a means of linking the electricity network in Greece and the other Balkan countries (which are currently isolated) to the Italian network and the rest of the interconnected European UCPTE network.

The project will entail laying a 160 km underwater cable at a depth of 1 000 m and constructing two 400 kV direct current overhead lines (45 km in Italy and 110 km in Greece) plus two substations for conversion between direct and alternating current at Galatina (Italy) and Aractos (Greece).

The scheme will cost approximately ECU 300 million, three quarters of which will be for the Italian side and one quarter for the Greek side. The ERDF has already granted aid totalling ECU 35 million as part of the Community's 1989-93 REGEN programme. This scheme could also qualify for support from the Interreg programme for 1994–99. Licensing procedures are in progress and prototype cables are being manufactured. The scheme is scheduled to come into operation by the end of 1997.

Electricity projects

Interconnection between France and Italy (b6)

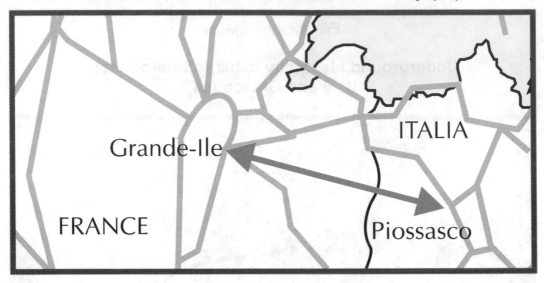

This project is of primordial interest for the two countries concerned. Italy is facing a need to import electricity, while France is keen to find markets for its production.

For this reason, a new 400 kV line is planned between the Grand Ile substation (Haute Savoie) and the Piossasco substation west of Turin, partly following the route of an existing line.

The estimated total cost of the project is between ECU 170 and 190 million. As the scheme is economically and financially viable, funding will pose no problem. Technically the project is ready and could be completed in two or three years. Nevertheless, there have been difficulties in obtaining the licences needed, particularly on the Italian side. These licences will depend on the environmental impact assessments now under way.

Electricity projects

Interconnection between Spain and Portugal (b10)

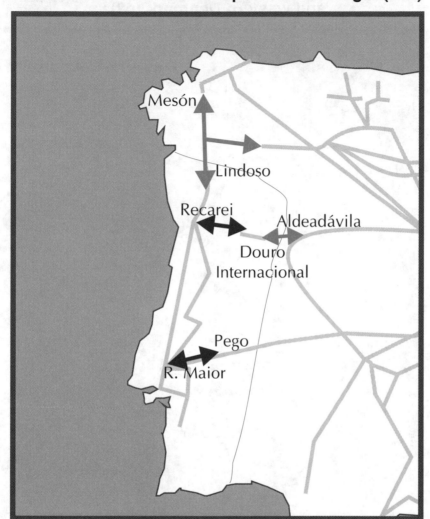

These three high-voltage lines are of great importance to the development of an integrated electricity system for the Iberian Peninsula and subsequent integration thereof into the Mediterranean circuit. In closer detail, the project consists of three interconnections, the first of which is the most important:

☐ north: Mesón — Cartelle — Lindoso — Recarrei (400 kV)
☐ north-east: Recarei — Douro International — Aldeadávila (400/220 kV)
☐ centre: Rio Maior — Pego (400 kV).

The total combined cost will be approximately ECU 130 million. As the project is extremely viable, no funding problems are feared. However, there are still a few minor problems concerning environmental protection and the licences needed.

In any event, classification of this major project as a 'project of Community interest' could speed up the work. Also, rapid completion of the new France — Spain (Cazaril — Aragon) line would add considerably to the value of this interconnection between Spain and Portugal.

Electricity projects

Underwater cable link between eastern and western Denmark (c2)

At the moment mainland Denmark is connected to the UCPTE network and the islands to the Nordel network. This connection between the networks in eastern and western Denmark will establish an additional electricity link between the EU and the Nordic countries, making fuller use of the two fossil-fuel fired and hydroelectric generating systems.

The project will consist of a 400 kV underwater and underground cable plus two substations for DC/AC conversion at Zealand and Funen.

The total cost will be approximately ECU 170 million. The project is of great strategic importance, but of limited financial viability.

The project is ready. The technical specifications will be published soon. The scheme is scheduled to come into operation by the end of 1997.

Gas projects
Introduction of natural gas in Greece (e6)

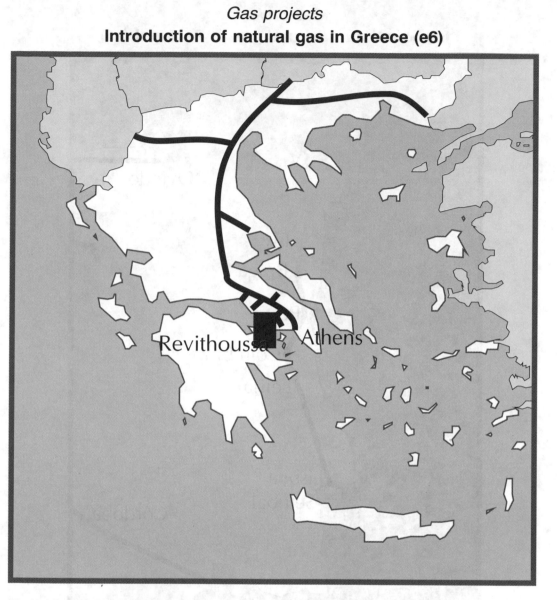

The introduction of natural gas will make it possible to diversify the energy supplies of Greece, which is heavily dependent on oil, and help to improve the environment, particularly in the Athens and Thessaloniki regions and in other cities. The scheme will allow more flexible power station siting and serve as a symbol of cohesion with the rest of the Union.

It entails laying a 510 km pipeline from the frontier with Bulgaria to the western Mediterranean coast of Athens, with various branches to the main centres of consumption, and constructing a LNG station at Revithoussa (near Athens).

The total cost (excluding the distribution network) will be between ECU 1 200 and 1 300 million. Up to ECU 400 million was invested between 1990 and 1993, with Community support from the ERDF totalling ECU 149 million, an EIB loan of USD 10 million and an ECSC loan of ECU 100 million. This project has already received support under the REGEN programme but needs further financial aid. It could also receive support from the new Interreg programme for 1994–99.

Construction of the main pipeline started in 1991 (380 km of pipeline have already been laid). All the work (pipelines and LNG station) is scheduled to be completed by 1998.

Gas projects
Introduction of natural gas in Portugal (e5)

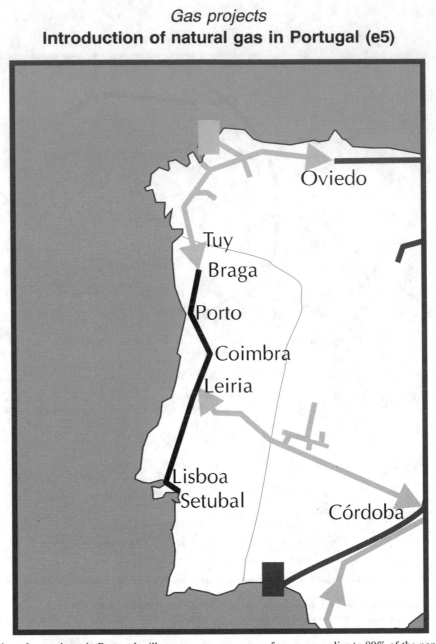

Introduction of natural gas in Portugal will open up a new source of energy supplies to 80% of the population and 85% of Portugal's industry. Use of this cleaner fuel will help to reduce the country's dependence on oil and have a positive impact on the environment.

The project entails laying a 370 km pipeline with a capacity of 2.5 billion m³/year between Setubal and Braga. The natural gas will be supplied by Algeria via the Maghreb pipeline currently under construction.

The project will cost ECU 440 million, to which the ERDF has already contributed aid totalling ECU 82 million. Additional aid could be granted under the new Interreg programme for 1994–99.

One third of the investment has been committed already. Final completion of the project is scheduled in 1996.

Gas projects
Interconnections between Spain and Portugal and introduction of natural gas in the Galicia and Extremadura regions of Spain (f6)

In order to introduce natural gas in Portugal, interconnections with Spain will have to be built to carry the natural gas from Algeria (southern interconnection) and, possibly, other destinations (northern interconnection) to increase the security of supply. At the same time the first of these pipelines will provide an opportunity to introduce natural gas in Extremadura and the second in Galicia.

The southern interconnection will entail laying a 430 km pipeline at a cost of approximately ECU 300 million between Cordoba (Spain) and Leiria (Portugal). This will also supply natural gas to Extremadura at an additional cost of ECU 37 million.

The northern interconnection, from Oviedo, will extend the Spanish network, already connected with France, to Galicia and Portugal at a cost of approximately ECU 460 million.

Gas projects
Algeria — Morocco — European Union pipeline (h4)

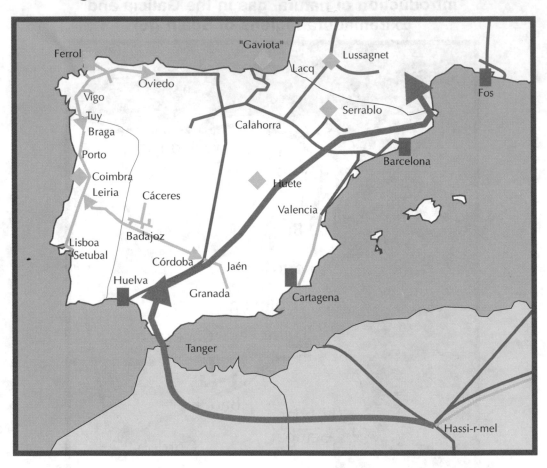

A new gas pipeline will be laid to supply natural gas from Algeria to Spain and Portugal in the first phase and to France and the rest of the European Union in the second phase. This will increase transmission capacity and diversify the supply routes for natural gas.

The pipeline will have a capacity of 18.5 billion m³/year, 8.5 billion of which will be used to double natural gas consumption in Spain and introduce this new fuel in Portugal. That will leave 10 billion m³ for new markets.

The 45 km crossing of the Straits of Gibraltar and the Tarifa/Cordoba pipeline will cost approximately ECU 450 million.

One third of the investment has already been committed. The scheme is scheduled for completion by the end of 1995.

Progress report on employment
Results of Mr Flynn's tour of capitals[1]

[1] SEC(94) 951 final.

Contents

Part 1

Introduction

This report has been prepared following the Tour of Capitals undertaken by Commissioner Flynn, at the request of the College, between February and June, during which discussions have been held, at this stage, with 11 national governments and the social partners at the national level.

The report also takes into account the reports received from Member States, within the framework of the Social Affairs Council, on progress in implementing suggestions of the White Paper, and the conclusions of the European Council (December 1993, Brussels) as far as the employment dimension is concerned. It also takes into account the results of discussions with Directors-General of the Member State Ministries, the work of the Economic Policy Committee, and results received from the Commission's Observatories. The contributions of the social partners have also been considered. Finally, the reports of the European Parliament and of the Economic and Social Committee; and discussions within the Council's Standing Committee on Employment have been taken into account.

Employment Trends

At the time of the European Council discussion of the White Paper in December 1993, unemployment had been rising continuously for almost three years following the downturn in economic growth which began in 1990. During 1993 output declined for the first time since 1975. The recession in output led to a reduction in employment in almost all parts of the Union.

As a result of the general fall in employment and the continued rise in working-age population, as well as in the participation of women, unemployment rose during 1993 in all Member States without exception. The average rate for the Union as a whole, including all of Germany, was 10.9%. By March 1994, average unemployment had reached 11% in the Union, implying that, overall, there were almost 17 million people out of work based on Eurostat labour force survey figures. (Registered unemployment in Member States totals 18.8 million.)

In general, unemployment rose more slowly during 1993 and, over the first four months of 1994, increased only marginally in the Union as a whole. However, despite the improved outlook for growth, increasing labour force participation rates mean that, unless efforts to increase the employment content of growth are strengthened, unemployment is unlikely to fall in the short-term.

Unemployment rates remain particularly high for young people under 25, averaging over 20% in the Community as a whole in March 1994. Long-term unemployment continues to be a serious problem in most parts of the Union, with an average of 42% of the unemployed having been out of work for one year or more in 1992 — although down from 45% in 1991.

A substantial reduction in unemployment requires that growth remains strong for many years, and becomes more employment creating. Growth prospects for 1994 and 1995 have improved, but success in translating this into employment growth will require continued, determined, structural adjustment efforts and careful macroeconomic management, both actions being mutually reinforcing.

Preliminary conclusions of tour

The White Paper strategy is a medium-term one. It cannot be expected to yield short-term successes, and certainly not to lead to any noticeable reduction in unemployment in a matter of months. Thus, progress needs to be judged at this stage primarily in terms of trends and changes in political positions, rather than concrete results.

The essential message is clear: all Member States, in their different ways, are seeking to introduce changes to their labour market policies, directly or indirectly related to the White Paper's suggestions. Some have now introduced interdepartmental machinery to pursue the White Paper and the Brussels conclusions. The White Paper has been carefully examined as a valuable point of reference in all Member States, including by social partners at national level.

However, the urgent need for collective reflection and coordinated action across the whole range of policies affecting the broad employment environment has not yet been realized. A fragmentary approach is still noticeable. Old and complex national regulations still remain in force in many Member States. The reforms in the employment systems adopted so far by Member States often appear incomplete and it is difficult at this stage to assess their wider impact. Most Member States now recognize, however, the need to build the long-term social consensus in favour of structural changes especially where they affect people's living and working conditions.

Member States generally recognize also that this search for consensus implies that greater labour market efficiency and long-run competitiveness is to be sought, not through a dilution of the European model of social protection, but through the adaptation, rationalization and simplification of regulations, so as to establish a better balance between social protection, competitiveness and employment creation.

Increased labour market flexibility means different things to different Member States, and needs to be analysed carefully, as the term 'deregula-tion' is often used with differing connotations. The starting point, for most Member States, is a large body of laws, regulations or collective arrangements. Their ending point, in terms of the nature and scale of change required, is, therefore, likely to differ widely — even after substantial review — particularly in terms of the degree of, and approach to, change in social protection. In analysing these differences between Member States, the strong traditions of social partners' involvement in many Member States has to be taken carefully into account. In this context, most Member States are concerned about balancing actions to enhance job creation and competitiveness with their commitment to maintain and not dismantle social protection.

Most Member States stress the need for a more dynamic contribution from the social partners at local and sectoral levels, and a stronger partnership between them and public authorities at those levels. At national level, some Member States recognize the importance of building greater complementarity between public policy and contractual negotiations.

At Union level, discussions with the social partners have continued within the framework of the social dialogue, with a particular focus on White Paper employment issues. The Council's Standing Committee on Employment has also discussed issues of work organization and working time in a positive way.

Among the social partners at national level, positive attitudes — reflected for instance in certain agreements — coexist with reticence to change. The need for far-reaching reform of the employment systems has yet to become generally accepted. Greater public awareness and acceptance that there are trade-offs between sacrifices in the short-term in exchange for the creation of more jobs will be necessary to ensure the adoption and implementation of these reforms.

Major political difficulties have been encountered by governments seeking to undertake reforms in this sense. Resistance from those who feel threatened by the changes is not compensated for by any obvious public support from those people who would benefit most, but who are largely disenfranchised or excluded from the labour market at present.

The White Paper stresses the need to dramatically widen access to work, to widen the concept of work, and to build a new solidarity. That solidarity has to be based on using productivity gains to create new jobs rather than increase incomes of those in employment, and to avoid the burden of change being borne only by those in the weakest position in society — the easiest, but least acceptable, way of increasing access to jobs.

In particular, the White Paper underlines the need to ensure that progress in achieving equal opportunities is further pursued, particularly in view of the increased participation rates of women, changing family structures and roles, and the need to maximize the potential of all the Union's human resources. In this respect, increased economic growth brings a positive and welcome improvement to the employment climate. However, there is a danger that it may offer an illusion of relief from the pressures for structural change, rather than being harnessed to work systematically towards the changes required in that better economic environment.

It will be very important to continually bring that message home to the Member States, if a serious reduction in unemployment is to be achieved throughout the Union. This is particularly important in view of demographic change, the increased public budget pressure it will bring, and the resultant need for stronger employment generation. For all these reasons, more attention needs to be focused on new jobs and the most promising sectors for employment growth.

The need to fundamentally alter, and update, the structure of incentives which influence the labour market is still not adequately recognized. Cooperation across Ministerial boundaries within Governments in the development of policies needs to be given greater priority. Further organizational and administrative changes will be needed if the implementation of the White Paper strategy is to be pursued effectively.

It is not only measures which need to be redesigned, it is also important for Member States to review the structures through which governments address employment problems. In this context, some Member States have developed, or are in the process of setting up, inter-ministry action on specific subjects. Also most Member States are already decentralizing the delivery of labour market (including training) measures as part of a move towards more active targeting of those at risk especially the long-term unemployed. Some are seeking to integrate services at local/regional level instead of the previously fragmented range of services available.

Union role

Policy development

The Union's employment objectives are supported, at Community level, by policy and action in the economic, industrial, technological and scientific fields. Completion of the internal market, action on research and development, and support to small and medium enterprise, have all brought added value to the Union's efforts to sustain and generate employment.

In recent months, the White Paper and Council focus on firm macroeconomic guidelines, the trans-European networks, and the exploitation of new technologies — particularly regarding telecommunication applications and biotechnologies — has further strengthened the ability of the Union to meet the challenges of competitiveness and job creation.

All of these advances in policy development and action are dependent for their success on the quality, creativity and flexibility of the workforce at all levels, which drives the development and delivery of the wealth and job creation process. In order to maximize the potential of this most important component, the Community focuses particularly on employment and related human resource issues through a range of policies and activities.

The responsibility for employment and human resource development lies with Member States. However, in redesigning national policies and systems in these fields, in the framework of the White Paper and Brussels Council Objectives, it will be of crucial importance to develop and maximize the added value of Unionwide action and mutual support, in order to fully exploit the diversity of Member State experience.

This means looking at the efficiency of different national systems in achieving employment objectives. It means looking at the possibilities to 'pick and mix' different elements of policy from different national systems. It also means the pursuit of increased compatibility between Member States' systems, so as to ensure that they do not develop in ways which conflict with overall Union employment objectives or standards, distort conditions of competition, or inhibit the development of free movement of people within the Union.

In this respect, the increased cooperation between the Member States and the Commission with regard to the White Paper is encouraging, but will need to be pursued much more systematically during the coming months.

Financial support

Much of what the Community does, in terms of financial and other resource support, has an impact on employment, through programmes and actions as diverse as research and development, infrastructure investment, education and training, and trade agreements.

A number of new developments such as the Fourth Framework Programme for research and development, a range of support mechanisms for small and medium enterprise, and such as Leonardo, with regard to education and training, will strengthen this effort.

A fundamental component of the Union's structural policies, and of its strategy to achieve the adjustments necessary for growth, competitiveness and employment, is its financial support for human resource development and labour market adjustment. Community Support Frameworks, under the Structural Funds, and accounting for more than ECU 40 billion of European Social Fund financing, are currently being negotiated for the period 1994–99. (1994–96, in the case of Objectives 2 and 4.)

Member State proposals, under Objectives 1, 3 and 4, were prepared and presented to the Commission before the White Paper was established. In the discussions on the Community Support Frameworks the Commission has, therefore, promoted a strategic approach based on three priority themes:

☐ improving access to and quality of education and initial training, especially through the implementation of 'Youthstart',

☐ increasing competitiveness and preventing unemployment by adapting the work-force to the challenge of change through a systematic approach to continuing training, including through implementation of 'Adapt',

☐ improving employment opportunities of those exposed to long-term unemployment and exclusion, though the development of a package of measures which form a pathway to reintegration, including through the 'Employment' Community Initiative.

Many Member States have endorsed this approach, but there is a need for them to carefully review their strategies for long-term investment in education and training so that they may compete effectively on the World stage, strengthened by a skilled and flexible work-force. The priority accorded to investment in human resources within the Union's structural policies needs to be reaffirmed.

It is essential to ensure that, within the framework of subsidiarity and partnership, Member States give full attention to these concerns, and that the Community Support Frameworks which are now being agreed retain sufficient flexibility to adapt action and financial efforts as needs unfold with the further implementation of the White Paper Strategy.

Follow-up

An important operational lesson of the first six months for governments is that there is a need to reinforce cooperation at national level — between the Ministries, agencies and Social partners concerned — and between the national level and the Union level.

Member States, and Employment and Social Affairs Ministers in particular, need to identify specific objectives and actions, both short and medium-term, within the framework of the Council mandate, in time for examination by the European Council in Essen in December 1994.

Efforts to develop positive actions for employment in the diverse areas of policy should continue to be carried out in the specialized Councils of Mininsters. Improved coordination of these efforts at Community level will increase their efficiency and intensity. In support of this process, the Commission will continue to collaborate closely with the Member States in mapping the employment situation. In this context, the 1994 Employment Report will be issued in the summer, and a comparative tabular picture of the situation across the Union is in preparation.

Part 2

Member State actions: executive summary

The European Council agreed to a series of priority actions within the general framework defined in common in the light of the White Paper. These were specified as follows:

☐ improving **education and training** systems. Continuing training is, in particular, to be facilitated so as to ensure ongoing adjustment of skills to the needs of competitiveness and to combating unemployment;

☐ improving **flexibility** within enterprises and on the labour market by removing excessive rigidities resulting from regulation as well as through greater mobility;

☐ examination, at enterprise level, of economically sound formulas for the **reorganization** of work; such measures must not be directed towards a general redistribution of work, but towards internal adjustments compatible with improved productivity;

☐ targeted reductions in the **indirect costs of labour** (statutory contributions), and particularly of less skilled work, in order to achieve a better balance between the costs of the various factors of production; fiscal measures possibly relating, *inter alia,* to the environment could be one of the means of offsetting a drop in social contributions, within a general context of stabilizing all statutory contributions and reducing the tax burden;

☐ better **use of public funds** set aside for combating unemployment by means of a more active policy of information, motivation and guidance of job-seekers through specialized agencies, whether public or private;

☐ specific measures concerning **young people** who leave the education system without adequate training;

☐ developing employment in connection with **meeting new requirements** linked to the quality of life and protection of the environment.

All Member States have taken actions in at least some of the seven target areas, with the majority developing actions in most. There are positive signs in a number of areas — notably in seeking to remove bureaucratic obstacles to change, in addressing problems of regulation, while maintaining minimum standards. Moreover, there is increased openness, and a willingness among Member States to discuss common problems and to exchange experience.

In general, Member State actions are still focused on managing unemployment problems, although they recognize the need to address employment issues in their wider context and to actively create jobs. More attention needs to focus on wide-ranging reform of government actions with respect to the interrelated issues of social protection, taxation and employment, on which there has been some useful action targeted on reducing the non-wage costs of the unskilled.

In areas such as those involving financial systems — changes in the incidence of taxation on employment, or changes in the use of social protection funds — it is recognized that such measures will take time. However, in that area in particular, policy will need to ensure that changes are pursued rather than allowed to flag in the face of difficulties or reduced pressures.

Education and training

Member States are continuing to sharpen the focus of their educational and vocational training policies with a view to improving long-term competitiveness, and ensuring a skilled and adaptable labour force. In all Member States there is an emphasis on standards, and in some on a more decentralized delivery and much greater involvement of the social partners.

Despite this progress, and despite the widespread recognition of the need for lifelong learning, action remains limited as regards continuous training. Some financial incentives have been provided and some collective agreements do make specific reference to work-force training. However, a more systematic, comprehensive, approach is needed along the lines proposed in the White Paper.

As regards meeting the need for new skills, the adoption of new technologies on a more widespread basis, diversifying career paths for women, and actions to cope with the consequences of large scale industrial change, action is often patchy and localized.

Improving flexibility

Member States have continued to take measures to introduce greater flexibility into the external labour market, particularly with regard to employment regulations covering contracts, notably with regard to part-time work. Redundancy and dismissals' legislation has been reformed in some Member States where they were particularly restrictive.

Employment protection has been increased in some Member States and some areas, in order to provide better minimum standards, for example with respect to maternity rights, part-time work and health and safety.

Some limited steps are being taken to promote occupational and geographical mobility, as well as European-wide information for job-seekers.

Member States continue to encourage wage restraint flexibility and decentralized negotia-

tions in their efforts to ensure that real income growth per employee remains below productivity growth, in order to encourage and assist employment growth.

Most Member States consider that internal flexibility is to be encouraged, within the overall industrial relations structure, but that it is essentially the responsibility of firms.

Work organization

There is considerable activity across the Member States in developing new patterns of working time as a means of increasing the number of jobs for a given level of output. In some cases this has active government support, in others it is contained more in collective or plant level agreements. Many large firms are restructuring working time as part of a wider restructuring of their organization.

Measures to remove obstacles to part-time working are being taken in most Member States where they still exist. Schemes contain many different options both to encourage existing employees, who so wish, to move to part-time working, as well as to create new possibilities. However, Member State policies do not always ensure of equal treatment of part-time and full-time work in all aspects.

Non-wage labour costs

In order to reduce the relative costs of labour and hence disincentives to recruitment, the White Paper recommends a move away (1 to 2% of GDP) from labour-based taxes and charges to taxes on non-renewable resources such as energy, capital, consumption, etc. The White paper also recommends that Member States address the current disincentives regarding less skilled workers' employment by adjusting taxation systems, especially when the overall effect of taxes and charges is regressive.

A number of Member States have already introduced modifications aimed at reducing the overall burden of taxes and social charges on labour. This has been done either across the board, or targeted on young people, the long-term unemployed, lower paid or less skilled workers, small and medium enterprises, or through enterprises providing training. Other Member States are considering a general lowering of taxes and charges rather than a restructuring. Certain taxes are very sensitive and divergences are to be avoided between Member States. For instance, some Member States favour increasing VAT revenues when others would rather reduce VAT rates for labour intensive sectors.

While there is widespread support for the idea of reducing non-wage labour costs in order to boost employment, the difficulties inherent in raising alternative revenues during a recession are equally evident.

Public funds

There has been an emphasis on improving the effectiveness of measures to help reintegrate the unemployed, and on making income support more conditional on proven action to seek work, undergo training or community work.

There is as yet, however, limited use made of schemes to 'top-up' low income from employment with income from social transfers, along the lines recommended in the White Paper.

Member States have sought to provide better support for the unemployed by developing the services of public employment agencies, and by lifting restrictions on, or legalizing, private employment agencies, where these were not previously allowed. A number of Member States have decentralized their employment agency operations, giving greater responsibility to the local and regional level.

Young people

Over the years, Member States have developed a variety of schemes and programmes to help young people, especially the 10% of young people who leave school each year without qualifications, to enter the labour market. They involve a variety of actions including guidance and counselling; support for job search; help in attaining numeracy and literacy; and basic training, often linked with workplace experience.

Member States are now tending to move towards more comprehensive programmes which integrate these activities and which target those facing the greatest difficulties. The Commission White Paper proposal for a specific Youthstart programme targeted at unqualified young people under 20 seeks to focus and reinforce this trend.

Recognizing the growing importance of skills, there is also a resurgence of interest in some Member States in apprenticeship training schemes. Most Member States are increasing the vocational content of education.

Developing new employment

Most Member States rely on commercially-driven activities, or conventional public services, as the source of employment creation. However, some specific initiatives have been taken in the Member States in order to promote new job opportunities, notably in local services, and often in the context of the social economy, along the lines recommended in the White Paper.

The potential of many other areas of job growth that were identified in the White Paper, such as arts and culture, tourism, and environmental protection, where public-private partnerships are generally needed to maximize their development, remain undersupported.

Moreover, there is little evidence of any more systematic attempts to monitor employment growth across all types of activity in ways which could help focus, and maximize, the impact of policy and resource support.

Member State actions in detail

Practically all Member States have undertaken extensive labour markets reforms in recent years, either in the form of new programmes or as part of an ongoing process of review and development. Member State progress in pursuing White Paper objectives will depend, therefore, on what has been achieved in recent years, and what is still in the pipeline, as well as on the content of recently announced changes or proposals.

This report presents Member State developments under the seven headings identified by the European Council. However, it is recognized that, at national level, these are generally seen as elements of integrated actions designed to alter the overall dimensions and focus of Member State employment policy systems, and that there is often overlap between the different elements.

Education and training

'improving education and training systems. Continuing training is, in particular, to be facilitated so as to ensure ongoing adjustment of skills to the needs of competitiveness and to combating unemployment'

All Member States have expressed their determination to improve the quality of education and vocational training, and to sharpen the focus of their policies in order to better meet the challenge of long-term competitiveness, and to provide a highly skilled, flexible and adaptable work-force. All Member States, moreover, underline the need to increase awareness that investment in the qualifications of the present and future work-force is as indispensable as investment in capital equipment and infrastructure. Special concern has been expressed by some Member States about the need for better coordination of the policies pursued by Education and Employment Ministries which generally have overlapping responsibilities with regard to vocational training. (Ireland, Spain.)

Across the Union, action to improve education and training systems and improve access to continuing training centres around three main issues: the development of the framework of vocational training policies; the promotion of life-long learning; and the need to meet the challenge of the rapid spread of new technology and industrial change.

Member States recognize that, while in the past measures have been responses to particular problems such as high unemployment amongst young people, increases in long-term unemployment and problems posed by industrial change, there is now a need for a more comprehensive longer-term strategy, to equip the work-force effectively for the single market. Even before the White Paper, Member States were in the process of major reforms of their education and training systems which address some of the issues raised in it.

While systems in the Member States are very different, many of the problems and challenges they face are the same, which points strongly to the need for Member States' policies to take account of developments in other parts of the European Union.

There is an overriding concern to improve quality and a variety of approaches are being used, including setting minimum legal standards (Germany), targets for qualification levels in the work-force (United Kingdom, France) and the setting of reference points for policy development (Luxembourg). There is also an increasing trend to decentralize the delivery of training to locally based structures, and to ensure a greater involvement of the private sector in the process (notably in France, Portugal, Denmark, the Netherlands, Luxembourg, Greece).

Most Member States now emphasize the need to put a higher premium on vocational qualifications, and to place them on a par with academic qualifications within the framework of a unified national system of certification, in place of existing disparate certification arrangements. Most Member States stress too the need for a closer association of the social partners with the design, management and delivery of training. Many Member States stressed the need for stronger action on recognition and transparency of qualifications to promote labour mobility.

So far as continuing training is concerned, all Member States are concerned to improve and extend access and participation, and stress the importance of in-company training with appropriate vocational assessment of workers, and also the links with local and regional authorities, especially in terms of forecasting skill needs and shortages.

The need for life-long learning is widely recognized in Member States. Measures to promote continuing training and life-long learning include promoting apprenticeship schemes (United Kingdom, France, the Netherlands, Belgium, Spain) (see section on young people), legal rights to training leave (Belgium, France), clauses in collective agreements (the Netherlands, Denmark, Germany), financial incentives (Belgium, Portugal, United Kingdom) and tax levies to finance training (France, Greece, Ireland).

There is some evidence of the introduction of tax incentives to encourage increased investment in human resources — through tax relief to companies, or financial assistance through loans or tax relief for individuals paying for their training and also help to small employers to invest in developing the skills of their employees (United Kingdom). However, no Member State has introduced generalized tax or other financial incentives to firms and individuals along the lines proposed in the White Paper.

Some measures are being taken to encourage individuals to take responsibility for their own training but, in the main, the emphasis rests in a more limited sense on occupational guidance to promote choice.

Furthermore, despite efforts to give priority to continuing training for the least qualified and the unemployed, and the creation of more incentives for this group (Denmark), there is evidence that access to continuing training is unequal, with highly qualified workers in large enterprises most likely to benefit. Although this problem is widely recognized, there remain significant barriers for large sections of the work-force to access to training. It also remains the case that, despite a range of measures in Member States to promote equal opportunities, women remain underrepresented in certain sectors and at senior levels of the economy.

At European level, the representatives of the trade unions have offered to negotiate a collective bargaining agreement so as to extend access to and participation in continuing training, and build on the previous joint opinions agreed within the framework of the social dialogue. At this stage, the employers' representatives have not taken up this offer.

Some steps are being taken (Denmark, Germany) to consider adult education and continuing training in its widest sense, in terms of acquiring key personal and social competences that can be effectively used in the workplace, although this concept is not widely developed. There are some signs (Denmark) of a new approach to the organization of working life, with a high degree of alternation between work, training and leave. Denmark has introduced an ambitious job rotation scheme which combines incentive for education and training breaks for employees, while increasing job training of unemployed people recruited as substitutes for those on training leave. Belgium, too, has a successful career break scheme. Apart from this, many issues concerning the organization of work and training remain largely unexplored across the Union.

Almost all Member States have responded positively in the presentation of their Community Support Framework to the opportunity presented by the new Objective 4 (European Social Fund) to develop new forms of anticipative training to help companies plan for structural change.

As far as the important issue of demand for new skills is concerned all Member States undertake research into likely developments of skill needs including at sectoral (France, Spain) and local level. However, there appears to be no focus in this research as to possible sources of new jobs. The use of new technology is becoming established practice in secondary education, but there is considerable variation in the way in which technology is transferred to the workplace. Some initiatives are being taken (Denmark, France), but there is a sense that the potential here has not been fully exploited. Policy responses to the need to adapt to industrial change are being developed, and range from specific action plans (Germany for the East, Spain, Belgium) to actions to support small firms (Denmark), or more general advice and support measures (United Kingdom).

There remains the key question of assessing the impact of the reforms and initiatives proposed or in place in Member States. The nature of the systems and the wide range of interests involved mean that this can only be done over time. However, work needs to continue to identify objectives, as well as qualitative and quantitative data to assess the effectiveness of policies.

Flexibility

'improving flexibility within enterprises and on the labour market by removing excessive rigidities resulting from regulation as well as through greater mobility'

In the Member State submissions prior to the White Paper, a lack of flexibility in European labour markets was identified as a general problem — in terms of the organization of working time, pay and mobility, and in terms of the matching of labour supply to the needs of the market. Member States saw the introduction of more flexibility as being centred on the way work is organized. It was considered that increased flexibility should also be reflected in the collective bargaining rules and systems.

Since the publication of the White Paper, Member States have continued to take measures within their own responsibilities to introduce greater flexibility, notably with regard to the external labour market. Action has covered legislation concerning redundancies and dismissals, and legislation and collective agreements concerning the form and content of labour market contracts, including working time.

In terms of flexibility, Spain is going furthest in the pursuit of labour market reforms with a wide-ranging programme designed to encourage recruitment by easing the process of labour market adjustment, and to reduce the segmentation of the market. This includes measures regarding working time, dismissals regulation, collective agreements and the negotiation process. The United Kingdom has followed a deregulation policy in this respect for some time, and further measures are proposed. The Netherlands also plans to relax regulations relating to the dismissal of staff, while continuing to uphold recourse to law. In Ireland, a task force on small businesses has recommended changes in regulations. This includes measures regarding working time, dismissal regulation, collective agreements and the negotiation process.

In terms of policy action by the Member States in general, however, most emphasis has been put on changes with regard to temporary and permanent employment contracts, and to the possibilities for undertaking part-time work. Recent measures include: greater flexibility with regard to fixed-term contracts in Spain, with particular regard to access for unemployed workers over 45; the possibility to renew fixed-term contracts, and to reduce notice periods for young people and the more highly paid in Belgium; the authorization of temporary employment agencies in a number of Member States (see under public funds); the extension of incentives to firms which use part-time workers (France); the abolition of some restrictions on part-time work in Spain, including new arrangements with regard to relating hours worked to social security; and a commitment to revise legislation in Ireland. In Germany, a law allowing fixed-term contracts and the 'loan' of temporary workers for up to nine months between firms is being extended until the year 2000.

In a number of Member States, employment protection has been increased by the following measures: longer notice periods in Denmark, improved rights to information for employees in Ireland and the United Kingdom, and in respect of maternity in the United Kingdom, as provided in EC Directives, additional protection in respect of unfair dismissal related to health and safety, and when exercising a statutory right. A recent ruling has also extended considerably the protection of part-time workers under United Kingdom law.

Some steps have been taken to promote occupational and geographical mobility — notably in Spain and Germany where, in the latter, European guidance centres have been established, with electronic mail facilities, aimed at encouraging European-wide mobility. Changes in job classification systems are proposed in Spain.

As regards internal flexibility, most Member States see this as a matter for individual firms. Many recognize the important contribution which can be made by improved education and training, and they therefore put emphasis on ensuring that such arrangements are made within the framework of collective agreements. The Dutch Government intends to focus on improving flexibility by training those with few educational qualifications. The Danish Government aims to promote internal flexibility through active labour market policies, in particular through the strengthening of education and training. (See also Work organization.)

Member States continue to encourage wage restraint flexibility and decentralized negotiations in their efforts to ensure that real income growth remains below inflation levels, in order to encourage and assist employment growth (see also Non-wage costs section).

Work organization

> 'examination, at enterprise level, of economically sound formulas for the reorganization of work; such measures must not be directed towards a general redistribution of work, but towards internal adjustments compatible with improved productivity'

The White Paper put great emphasis on the potential employment benefits of more flexible patterns of working time, of reduced average working hours, and of part-time work (with certain conditions). Interest across Member States in developing new patterns of working time as a means of increasing the number of jobs for a given level of output is widespread, but variable.

In some Member States, notably Belgium, France and Germany, there is strong support at government level. In other Member States, such as the Netherlands, while governments are positive, they consider that it is more appropriate that actions are contained in collective agreements or in plant level agreements. The Netherlands, is, however, proposing a new working hours act which would simplify legislation. In the United Kingdom and Ireland there is less interest in working-time reductions, as such, as a policy instrument, although flexible options already exist and are generally promoted, and Ireland is committed to the introduction of a national voluntary scheme on work-sharing.

The issues addressed are varied. In some cases, interest centres on the annualization of working hours, as in France, where there is a very strong debate at all levels on this issue. Various incentives for employers to reduce individual working hours or introduce part-time working are now in place, or being developed. Belgium has also introduced a framework plan which puts the emphasis on choice and experimentation, and which outlines eight possible formulas for work sharing. In Germany the emphasis is on the promotion of part-time work, while safeguarding standards. The German Government believes that increased use of part-time arrangements is the best way of sharing available work.

More generally, many large firms — national and multinational alike — are restructuring their working time as part of a much larger restructuring within their organizations, with the emphasis on decentralization. Examples include car manufacturers in Germany, agreements in the German chemical industry and the Dutch retail industry. One major company has now agreed that overtime will no longer be paid, but annual working time will be reduced and additional staff recruited.

A particular focus of policy in most Member States concerns part-time work, and measures to remove obstacles to part-time working are being taken in most Member States where such obstacles still exist. These schemes contain many different options both to encourage existing employees, who so wish, to move to part-time working, as well as to create new jobs.

The level of part-time working varies widely across the Union, but is generally higher in the north. However, in Germany, part-time work has not been that high, and while responsibility for the creation of part-time jobs is seen to lie with firms, the government is conducting a major publicity campaign in order to bring the benefits of part-time work to the attention of managers.

German law provides protection for part-time workers against discrimination and provides other safeguards, for example with regard to unemployment benefits. All posts in the public services are, by law, open to part-time workers. Since 1992 it has been possible to combine part-time work with a pension. In most Member States, equal treatment of part-time and full-time workers is not guaranteed however, in relation to social security.

In Spain, part-time working is to be allowed in the public service and other restrictions on part-time work abolished. Belgium has also introduced measures allowing small and medium enterprises to derogate from specific restrictions on the length of part-time working.

In Italy, solidarity contracts are being used more widely than before with reduced working hours subsidised by the *cassa integrazione* to develop part-time work. A new work-sharing/training measure in Portugal provides for the temporary replacement of employees by unemployed people undergoing training. Denmark has strengthened and extended its schemes to create possibilities of leave of absence, as part of a broad drive to upskill the work-force. Best known is its job rotation programme which offers employment possibilities for the long-term unemployed when employees take career breaks.

Non-wage labour costs

'targeted reductions in the indirect costs of labour (statutory contributions), and particularly of less skilled work, in order to achieve a better balance between the costs of the various factors of production; fiscal measures possibly relating, *inter alia*, to the environment could be one of the means of offsetting a drop in social contributions, within a general context of stabilizing all statutory contributions and reducing the tax burden'

With regard to the non-wage component of labour costs, in order to reduce the relative costs of labour and hence disincentives to recruitment, the White Paper made two recommendations. Firstly, it recommended a move away (1 to 2% of GDP) from labour-based taxes and charges to taxes on non-renewable resources such as energy, capital, consumption, etc. Secondly, it recommended that Member States address the current disincentives regarding less skilled workers' employment by adjusting taxation systems, especially when the overall effect of taxes and charges is regressive.

A number of Member States have already introduced modifications aimed at reducing the overall burden of taxes and social charges on labour. This has been done either across the board (Luxembourg) or targeted on different categories — young people, long-term unemployed, lower paid or less skilled workers, small and medium enterprises, or through enterprises providing training (Belgium, Spain, France, United Kingdom).

Similar steps are following in Ireland where the reduction of non-wage costs has been described as the single most important contribution to reducing the costs of low-skilled work. Most Member States who have pursued these policies have done so as part of wider labour market restructuring plans.

Other countries are showing considerable interest in this approach, including in the Netherlands, where calculations of the potential increase in employment have been made, and new measures are coming into effect. Luxembourg has also proposed a reduction in employers' social security contributions.

Other Member States are considering a general lowering of taxes and charges rather than a restructuring. Certain taxes are very sensitive and there is a recognition of the need to avoid divergences between Member States. For instance, some Member States favour increasing VAT revenues when other would rather reduce VAT rates for labour-intensive sectors.

Governments have pursued the reduction in charges most rigorously where employment taxes are high, most notably in Belgium and France. However, the trend is not universal and some Member States, notably Greece, Denmark and the United Kingdom, have increased employment-based taxes, or plan to do so, although generally only to a small degree or in circumstances where the tax rates are currently very low. Differences in policy are, therefore, largely explained by the differences in current levels of employment taxes (notably employers' social security contributions) between Member States.

However, there are large differences in initial starting positions and in financial pressures on government budgets among Member States. Some Member States make provisions for a

reduction of indirect labour costs: this reduction amounts to 0.4% of GDP (1994) in two cases and between 2 and 3% (long-term) in another. In this respect it would be helpful if Member States were to share information and their experience in this field. This exchange of information and experience has just begun.

While there is widespread support for the idea of reducing non-wage labour costs in order to boost employment, the difficulties inherent in raising alternative revenues, especially in recession, is equally recognized. The information received so far makes it difficult to quantify (as a percentage of GDP) the global effects of these measures and even more difficult to quantify compensatory measures (reducing public expenditure, increasing tax revenues from non-labour sources, etc.).The absence of sufficient compensation could lead to increasing public deficits, at least cyclically.

With regard to the adoption of Eco-taxes as a means of paying for employment based tax reductions, as recommended in the White Paper, Member States are somewhat varied in their response from being generally in favour in the northern Member States of the Union — in particular Denmark, the Netherlands, Belgium and Germany, to being broadly open, as in Ireland, and less sure in the south, for example in Spain, although Greece is open to a gradual move in this direction.

Public funds

> **'better use of public funds set aside for combating unemployment by means of a more active policy of information, motivation and guidance of job-seekers through specialized agencies, whether public or private'**

The White Paper highlighted four particular issues in terms of the use of public funds regarding unemployment: the efficiency of labour market measures to reintegrate the unemployed; the role of the employment services; the need to restructure national government income support schemes in ways which enable income from work to be topped up with income from social security; and the need to widen the concept of work in ways which bring more people into the formal labour market.

In terms of improving the effectiveness of measures, emphasis is increasingly being put on early intervention in order to avoid unemployed people becoming long-term unemployed. France and the United Kingdom have actions built around interviews with the unemployed, and schemes to identify options for the unemployed are being strengthened in Denmark and the Netherlands. Germany has launched large scale schemes aiming to retain jobs in the eastern *Länder*.

Personalized counselling is increasingly seen as important, especially in northern Member States, with emphasis on improving the ability of the unemployed to compete, and to matching them to available jobs.

Member States have sought to provide better support for the unemployed by developing the services of public employment agencies, and by legalizing private employment agencies where these were not previously allowed — in Spain and, later, Italy and Germany. Limited remaining restrictions on private agencies — United Kingdom and the Netherlands — are also being abolished.

Many countries have changed, or are changing, the way in which the employment services work, with the introduction of self-service schemes, with closer contacts between the employment and social security offices and with further development of job club models.

There is still an ongoing debate, however, in some Member States, about the merits of integrating employment offices and benefit offices — the advantages of a 'one-stop shop' for clients, as against conflicts of objectives. In France, separate employment offices for young people are foreseen.

A number of Member States — Belgium, France, Spain, Denmark, the Netherlands, Greece — have promoted a decentralized approach, although the degree of autonomy given

to the local level can vary widely. In France and Denmark, in particular, emphasis is put on integrated local or regional coordination. Improvements in employment services in Denmark are considered to be due to the involvement of local authorities.

While it is widely recognized that the costs of so-called passive measures (income support) outweigh the costs of so-called active measures (training and job creation), by a factor of 2 to 1 in most Member States, there is seen to be only limited scope for transfer in the short-term, although there is something of a tightening up of expenditure in a number of cases.

Various steps are being taken, however, to shift passive measures of income support into more active measures. A number of Member States have experimented with a range of intermediate labour market models, often initiated at local level. In Germany, a new instrument, of limited duration, which activates unemployment benefits as wages subsidies has been introduced for the new *Länder,* and Denmark has introduced changes in its unemployment compensation system which strengthen the rights of the unemployed but at the same time encourage their placement in various activities. France has various schemes to encourage companies to take on unemployed people. The Netherlands is also considering action along these lines. Many issues remain to be resolved here, in terms of acceptability and nature of measures, including those of mutual or respective rights and responsibilities between government and individual, perceptions of support and policing, and credibility with regard to quality of programmes.

There is, as yet, limited use made of schemes to 'top-up' income from employment with income from social transfers, along the lines recommended in the White Paper, and which was intended to expand employment opportunities at the bottom end of the labour market and escape from problems of poverty traps. It is not clear whether existing, somewhat experimental, measures will be evaluated in ways that will enable Member States to decide whether or not to transform them into mainstream actions. At present, the interaction of systems very often create barriers rather than pathways to employment.

Young people

'specific measures concerning young people who leave the education system without adequate training'

Over the years, Member States have developed a variety of schemes and programmes to help young people entering the labour market, and in particular to help reintegrate the young unemployed. They involve guidance and counselling, support for job search, help in attaining numeracy and literacy and basic training often linked with workplace experience.

Within this, there is little evidence of special new measures designed to eliminate basic illiteracy, as well as the lack of other basic skills, on the part of school-leavers.

Virtually all Member States, however, have taken, or are now taking, steps to ensure that all young people are offered a sound, broadly-based initial vocational training, and most Member States have welcomed the idea of Youthstart as a further stimulus to national efforts. A wide-ranging selection of measures targeting young people has been introduced in many Member States over the last few years. However, the range of schemes sometimes makes it difficult to perceive how the individual finds his or her way through the systems, and some simplification could be useful.

More specifically, most Member States have recently committed themselves to:

☐ revitalize and extend the coverage of their apprenticeship system, improving quality and standards, including the work-based component;

☐ review their arrangements for vocational guidance, though without much evidence of the need to examine the links between such services and employment/placement services, whether public or private;

☐ review the training of trainers and instructors and their qualifications;

☐ a number have also sought to raise the status of vocational education in the shools (Belgium, United Kingdom, Spain, Ireland) in particular through providing access to further and higher education through vocational education;

☐ develop further the bridges between the worlds of school and work, including the introduction of more opportunities for work experience;

☐ experiment with the introduction of credits for young people (having left full-time compulsory education) to choose an approved course;

☐ encourage active partnerships between higher education and industry, including the two-way transfer of staff between institutions of higher education and companies.

Some Member States have set specific targets for increasing the numbers of young people in further and higher education (Spain, Portugal, United Kingdom) as well as actions to raise attainment rates before leaving the education system.

Several Member States (for example, Ireland, Denmark) refer to the importance of foreign-language teaching, and the need to encourage a spirit of enterprise among young people so as to develop skills to support job creation and economic development. Most have introduced the use of technology into the school curriculum.

Member States are now tending to move towards programmes which integrate many of these activities and which target those facing the greatest difficulties. More than 5 million young people in the Union have no formal qualifications; up to 10% of young people leave school without qualifications each year; and another 10 to 20% enter the labour market with only a lower secondary qualification.

Member States have reacted positively to the Commission White Paper proposal for a specific

Youthstart programme targeted at unqualified young people under 20.

All Member States have some form of youth guarantee scheme to help disadvantaged young people, ranging from a loosely connected series of separate measures, to a 'guided pathway' approach. A more comprehensive model is now emerging.

The first approach has been the most common, encompassing various elements such as: guidance/counselling; support for job search; help in attaining numeracy and literacy; pre-vocational and vocational training, often linked with workplace experience; adapted training courses or work-based programmes, but in relatively unrelated ways.

The 'guided pathway' approach has developed in order to smooth the transition from education to training to working life by creating structures with the appropriate capacity: to identify and connect with the target group of young people; motivate and engage them in developing individualized plans; provide appropriate access to all the individual elements that are needed. A number of Member State programmes now have features of this approach — the Education For All initiative (Germany); Youth reach (Ireland, Luxembourg); *Crédit formation individualisé* (France); Youth work guarantee (the Netherlands); Youth training (United Kingdom); The employment and training organization in Flanders (Belgium).

While such approaches bring greater clarity, there are moves to develop even more comprehensive systems with a proactive, preventive approach. In the Netherlands, a broad programme to prevent drop-out and ensure that a qualification is enjoyed by all was launched in 1993.

The Commission White Paper proposal, Youthstart, is aimed along these lines with a view to providing a stimulus to developing a comprehensive Communitywide approach to helping unqualified young people under 20. Measures proposed in the Leonardo programme will also provide support. Youthstart is intended to support schemes built on a range of minimum standards, key features of which are ensuring a coherent link with the labour market, recognized, marketable, qualifications and addressing personal and institutional barriers to labour market participation.

With regard to young people leaving schooling at secondary level, an important trend is the resurgence of interest in Member States in the use of apprenticeship training schemes (United Kingdom, Ireland, Spain, the Netherlands) as advocated in the White Paper. New efforts are also being made to develop measures such as recruitment subsidies (Belgium, France), on-the-job work experience (Italy), and quasi-public jobs at local level (Denmark).

Developing new employment

'developing employment in connection with meeting new requirements linked to the quality of life and protection of the environment.

Most Member States rely on commercially-driven activities or conventional public services, as the source of employment creation. However, many specific initiatives have been taken in the Member States in order to promote the development of new job opportunities, particularly at local level. However, such initiatives vary enormously in scale, nature and focus — depending, in part, on the perceived role of Member States' governments in relation to the process of employment creation.

However, in all countries, local public authorities, non-governmental organizations, regional trade union organizations and individuals are directly involved in numerous job creation schemes, which aim to respond to new needs as well as to provide employment. Activities include jobs connected with social services (child care, assistance to the elderly, handicapped persons or families, and support for young people in difficulty); the improvement of the quality of life (local public transport, security, housing, the revitalization of urban areas and community development); arts, culture, heritage, tourism and audiovisual activities; and environmental protection (investment in clean-up and waste management, pollution control, water, protection and maintenance of the countryside).

Measures taken to support such initiatives are very diversified. Sometimes they may form part of large sectoral policies — for example tourism in Ireland and Greece, cultural activities in the United Kingdom and France, information technology actions in Spain, Denmark and Ireland, environmental protection in Denmark, Luxembourg and Germany, and urban renewal in Portugal, Italy, the Netherlands and Belgium. In other cases, measures may respond to more local concerns such as housing projects, services to persons, transport, and moves away from institutional care systems.

Some Member States — notably France, Ireland, Germany, Denmark and Belgium — are seeking to promote more local level employment creation, by direct means, including the provision of vouchers for service jobs for families (France and Belgium), and by rural community economic development actions in tourism and education (Spain, Greece, Italy).

Important as these actions are in total, their diversity and multiplicity often means that they are less visible and less appreciated than more grandiose schemes, and their employment and social cohesion benefits underestimated. Government finance is, however, often involved in such projects, and local level employment offices and training agencies frequently have very close contacts with employers and the voluntary sector. Moreover, most Member States have, or have experimented with in the past, schemes to promote self-employment or very small businesses (for example, France, Belgium, and the United Kingdom).

However, since national governments are not always directly involved in these activities, their importance, and the benefits to be gained by developing local capacity to engage in these activities, is not always fully appreciated.

Thus, Member States do not seem to be exploiting the potential of these diverse sectors in any strategic way and systematic action to assess the potential of these sectors, and to promote employment growth in them, is generally lacking.

In short, local level employment creation activity abounds but the potential, and need, to develop many of the new areas of job growth that were identified in the White Paper — such as local services, arts and culture, tourism, and environmental protection — remains to be exploited, as does the potential for various forms of public-private partnership or social economy activity.

Extracts of the conclusions of the Presidency of the Corfu European Council

(24 and 25 June 1994)

White Paper

In December 1993 the European Council in Brussels adopted a plan of action based on the Commission White Paper on a medium-term strategy for growth, competitiveness and employment. It underlined that a healthy and open economy as well as an economy geared to solidarity were essential prerequisites for the successful implementation of this plan.

Signs of economic recovery are now being confirmed and non-inflationary economic growth is returning. The European Council considers it essential that the improvement in the economic situation should not lead to a slackening of efforts to promote structural adjustment in Europe but should instead be exploited to speed up essential reforms, particularly in the field of employment, where the situation is still very worrying.

The successful conclusion of the Uruguay Round within the guidelines set out by the European Council has created an international trade policy environment which can provide effective support for economic recovery and job creation. The European Council calls on the Community institutions and Member States to do everything necessary to complete ratification in time to ensure the entry into force before 1 January 1995. The European Union will play an active role in efforts to ensure that the new World Trade Organization can effectively carry out its task of ensuring observance of the rules drawn up jointly and promote progress in combating unfair trade conditions. Environmental and social issues will also have to be discussed in this context.

The European Council on the basis of a report from the President of the Commission had an in depth discussion on the different elements of the Action Plan decided in the Brussels European Council.

The European Council puts particular emphasis on the following points which should give new impetus in the follow-up debate on the White Paper.

(i) Encouragement of reforms in Member States intended to improve the efficiency of the systems of employment.

(ii) Specific measures with regard to fully exploiting the employment potential of small and medium-sized enterprises.

(iii) Reinforced coordination of research policy.

(iv) Rapid implementation of high priority trans-European projects in the field of transport and energy.

(v) Fully exploiting the possibilities and opportunities offered by the information society.

(vi) Encouragement of the new model of sustainable development including the environmental dimension.

1. Improving the employment situation

A sound macroeconomic environment is a *sine qua non* for success in the fight against unemployment (see point 5).

The resumption of economic growth will not of itself suffice to settle the problem of unemploy-

ment, which requires structural reforms both at the level of Member States and of the Union.

The European Council considers that increases in productivity for the rest of this century should be dedicated primarily to investments and jobs. This objective should be implemented in a spirit of solidarity and taking special account of those in society who are in the weakest position. The European Council stresses the need to maximize the potential of human resources.

The European Council reviewed, on the basis of a report from the Commission, the initiatives under way in the Member States in accordance with the general objectives defined in December 1993. The European Council noted progress in these areas but considered that the efforts undertaken so far, though appreciable, still fall a long way short of what is necessary. It encourages Member States in order to win the battle for jobs to take further steps to implement the objectives set out in December. In particular:

☐ with regard to education and training, the European Council concurs with the Commission's recommendation that a more systematic and comprehensive approach will be needed in many Member States, in particular with regard to continuing training. At the Community level the European Council welcomes the agreement in principle by the Council on the two new education and training programmes (Leonardo and Socrates) and invites the Council and the European Parliament to finalize the decisions on this programme before the end of the year.

☐ as regards measures to encourage employment, the European Council notes the Commission recommendation concerning the reduction of non-wage labour costs, mainly on the less skilled. In this framework, the European Council underlines that further steps should be pursued, consistent with the objective of budgetary consolidation.

Accordingly, the European Council takes note of the discussion on the CO_2/energy tax issues and underlines the need to ensure that environmental costs are better reflected throughout the economy.

☐ as regards the promotion of economically sound formulas for the organization of work, the European Council notes the need to remove obstacles to part-time work and in general to promote new forms of organization of work.

☐ with regard to developing new employment in connection with meeting new requirements linked to the quality of life and protection of the environment, the European Council notes that a number of initiatives have been taken but many of the new areas of job growth that were identified in the White Paper remain to be exploited. The European Council underlines the importance of the study to be prepared by the Commission before the next European Council on this subject.

☐ with regard to young people, the European Council considers that additional emphasis should be given to those young people who are facing the greatest difficulties. It attaches high importance to ensuring as far as possible that young people can move from education into work; in this context it welcomes the Commission's Youthstart programme.

To support these efforts the European Council invites the Social Affairs Council, the Ecofin Council and the Commission, on the basis of information collected by the Commission, to keep progress in this area under constant review. The Council will report to the European Council in Essen on national experiences which have had positive effects on employment, analysing the reasons for their success, and define appropriate policy recommendations for adapting current policies.

Efforts to promote youth employment and to combat long-term unemployment should be given particular priority in the work of the Council.

Finally the European Council invites the Commission to renew its efforts towards assuring the necessary social dialogue, making full use of the new possibilities available in the Treaty on European Union and in particular of the provisions of the protocol annexed to it.

2. The internal market, competitiveness and small and medium-sized enterprises

The smooth operation of the internal market is essential if the economy is to be competitive and dynamic. This means that the delays in transposing certain important Directives on public contracts, insurance, intellectual property and company law at national level must be remedied. Furthermore, it is essential that the basic principles of the single market should be extended to those areas, such as energy and telecommunications, which are still only partly covered by it while ensuring that the public service and town and country requirements in these sectors are also safeguarded.

The single market is implemented with due regard to environmental problems. The safeguard of important national environmental protection measures shall be secured in this context.

The single market is a fundamental aspect of Community construction but it is not an end in itself, as was already pointed out in the conclusions of the Rhodes European Council in 1988. It should be used to serve the welfare of all, in accordance with the tradition of social progress established in the history of Europe. The policy of the Union, alongside the policies of the Member States, should foster the affirmation of this social dimension. In the view of the Member States concerned, the recent agreement in the Council under the provisions of the Social Protocol concerning information and consultation of workers in multinational enterprises constitutes significant progress towards the realization of this objective. Further advances on the same basis, including efforts aimed at avoiding social exclusion, are essential in a society in rapid transformation. The European Council also welcomed the recent agreements in the Council on the protection of young workers as well as the creation of the agency for health and safety at work.

Small and medium-sized enterprises make a major contribution to growth and job creation and they should be able to benefit more from all the opportunities offered by the single market. The European Council welcomed the implementation by the Council of its orientations concerning interest rate subsidies for SMEs and that the Commission has decided to devote ECU 1 billion for the period 1994–99 for a Community initiative programme to help small and medium-sized enterprises adapt to the internal market and to the new competitive environment. It also noted with interest the recent Commission initiative for an integrated programme in favour of small and medium-sized enterprises, including action to simplify legislation and reduce administrative burdens on such enterprises, and the initiative of the Portuguese Prime Minister on the local dimension of the internal market and the initiatives taken by Ireland in the areas of social partnership and local development. The European Council considers that local development initiatives offer considerable potential for reinforcing the economic and social fabric of the European Union and for creating jobs. They are an essential element of the new model of development mentioned in the White Paper and will help to preserve cultural diversity within the Union. The European Council notes the Commission's intention, within the framework of the report on new potential sources of employment to be submitted to the European Council in Essen, to draw up a detailed inventory of the various actions at Community level to foster local development and local employment initiatives, particularly those concerning microenterprises and handicraft industries. This inventory will be accompanied by the proposals deemed necessary to enhance the consistency and the effectiveness of those actions.

Regarding scientific and technological research, the European Council expects that the recent decision on the ambitious 1994–99 framework programme, to which considerable funding has been allocated, will be followed up without delay by the rapid adoption of specific sector programmes. In this context the information sector and biotechnology are of particular importance. It also invites the Council to pursue a more systematic coordination of Community and national research policies and invites the Commission to take any useful initiatives to promote such coordination.

Lastly, the European Council expressed its conviction that the elimination of unnecessary legal and administrative burdens on business and making Community and national legislation simpler are important aspects of improving the competitiveness of the European economy. It welcomes the fact that the Commission is pursuing its efforts to simplify existing Community legislation and will reinforce its cost/benefit examination of proposed Community legislation. The Commission also intends to launch a process of examining the impact of existing Community and national legislation on employment and competitiveness. With regard to these latter aspects the European Council welcomes the establishment by the Commission of a group composed of independent persons to assist it in this task and attaches high importance to its work.

As regards subsidiarity the Council welcomes the progress made so far by the Commission in acting on the report of December 1993 and notes the Commission's undertaking to give a full report to Essen.

3. Trans-European networks for transport, energy and environmental projects

The single market will produce all the expected positive effects to benefit citizens and firms only if it can rely on effective trans-European networks for transport and energy. The European Council welcomed the work achieved so far by the group chaired by Mr Christophersen in accordance with the mandate given last December.

On the basis of the group's report, the European Council has agreed on a first priority list of 11 major transport projects, set out in Annex I. As far as the energy sector is concerned the European Council took note of the projects listed in Annex II and requested the Christophersen group to continue its work examining in particular their economic viability. The Member States involved are asked to make every effort to ensure that all the transport projects whose preparation is sufficiently advanced are started up immediately and that the others are started up as far as possible during 1996 at the latest by accelerating administrative, regulatory and legal procedures. The European Council invites the Commission to take all useful initiatives in this respect including the convening, where appropriate, of project seminars aimed at coordinating the activities of all parties involved.

The European Council also attaches importance to the other important transport projects which are set out in the interim report.

The European Council calls on the Christophersen group together with the representatives of the acceding States to continue their work on the basis of the mandate proposed in the group's report studying further the extension of the trans-European networks to neighbouring countries (in particular to Central and East European countries and to the Mediterranean Basin) and to prepare a final report to the European Council in Essen. It also asks the Christophersen group to examine the question of relevant networks in the field of the environment.

As regards financing of networks, the European Council confirms that measures will be taken, if proved necessary, in order that priority projects do not run into financial obstacles which would jeopardize their implementation. It noted the conclusions of the Ecofin Council and the studies carried out by the Commission. This question will continue to be examined by the Christophersen group and in the Ecofin Council until the Essen European Council, taking account of the specific characteristics of each project, the leading role of private funding and the judicious use of existing Community resources.

The Council will be informed if it appears that the achievement of certain projects is threatened for financial reasons linked to insufficient profitability — for example because of the length of investments or environmental constraints. The

Council will immediately consider with the Commission and the EIB the appropriate responses, within the limits set by the financial perspectives.

4. The information society

The European Council took note of the report from the group of leading figures representing the industry, operators and users who have been examining the various aspects of this question under the chairmanship of Mr Bangemann. The European Council considers that the current unprecedented technological revolution in the area of information opens up vast possibilities for economic progress, employment and the quality of life, while simultaneously representing a major challenge. It is primarily up to the private sector to respond to this challenge, by evaluating what is at stake and taking the necessary initiatives, notably in the matter of financing. The European Council, like the Commission, considers that the Community and its Member States do however have an important role to play in backing up this development by giving political impetus, creating a clear and stable regulatory framework (notably as regards access to markets, compatibility between networks, intellectual property rights, data protection and copyright) and by setting an example in areas which come under their aegis. The European Council agreed in general with the areas of application set out by the group (teleworking, distance learning, network for universities and research centres, telematic services for SMEs, road traffic management, air traffic control, health care networks, electronic tendering, administrative networks and city information high-

ways). The importance of linguistic and cultural aspects of the information society was also stressed by the European Council.

The European Council, having noted the findings of the Bangemann group, considers that the importance and complexity of the issues raised by the new information society justify the setting up of a permanent coordination instrument to ensure that the various parties involved, both public and private, are working along the same lines. This coordination instrument, to be set up as soon as possible, should be based on the appointment in each Member States of a person responsible at ministerial level for coordinating all aspects of the subject (political, financial and regulatory) with a view *inter alia* to ensuring a coordinated approach in the Council. The Commission will act similarly.

At the level of the Community, the necessary regulatory framework has to be established as soon as possible. The European Council invites the Council and the European Parliament to adopt before the end of the year measures in the areas already covered by existing proposals. It also invites the Commission to establish as soon as possible a programme covering the remaining measures needed at the Community level.

The European Council will assess progress at its meeting in Essen.

5. The macroeconomic environment

Regarding major economic trends, the European Council notes first of all that the Member States have broadly followed the guidelines laid down by the European Council in December 1993. Inflation, which is in the process of being overcome, a return to exchange rate stability and an incipient reduction of public deficits are

creating a sound basis for future growth and favouring the convergence of economies towards the criteria laid down in the Maastricht Treaty for the final stage of EMU. These efforts must be continued in order to consolidate the fall in short-term interest rates and to reverse the recent upward trend of long-term interest rates, all of which are essential conditions for stimulating investment and creating jobs.

For all these reasons the European Council endorses the economic policy guidelines contained in the report submitted by the Ecofin Council in accordance with Article 103 of the EC Treaty. It invites the Council to finalize the guidelines in the light of the conclusions of this European Council with regard to the implementation of the White Paper in general.

Annex I

List of high priority transport projects adopted by the European Council

Projects	Countries involved

Projects   **Countries involved**

High-speed train combined transport north-south   I/A/D
    Brenner axis Verona — Munich — Nuremberg — Erfurt
    — Halle/Leipzig — Berlin

High-speed train Paris — Brussels — Cologne —Amsterdam —London
    The following sections of the project are included
    Belgium: F/B border — Brussels — Liège — B/D border   B
    Brussels — B/NL border
    United Kingdom: London — Channel Tunnel Access   UK
    Netherlands: B/NL border — Rotterdam — Amsterdam   NL
    Germany: Aachen[1] — Cologne — Rhine/Main   D

High-speed train south
    Madrid — Barcelona — Perpignan — Montpellier   E/F
    Madrid — Vitoria — Dax   E/F

High-speed train east

The following sections of the project are included[2]
    Paris — Metz — Strasbourg — Appenweier — Karlsruhe   F/D
    with junctions to Metz — Saarbrücken — Mannheim   F/D
    and Metz — Luxembourg   F/L

Betuwe line: Combined transport/conventional rail   NL/D
    Rotterdam — NL/D border — Rhine/Ruhr[1]

High-speed train/combined transport France —Italy   F/I
    Lyons — Turin

Motorway Patras — Greek/Bulgarian border/   GR
jointly with the west-east motorway corridor: Via Egnatia
Igoumenitsa — Thessaloniki — Alexandroupolis — Ormenio/
Kipi

---

[1] Ongoing construction support already provided at Community level.

[2] The extension to Frankfurt is already under construction; as regards the further extension to Berlin the maturity of the project is not advanced enough.

Motorway Lisbon — Valladolid	P/E
Cork — Dublin — Belfast — Larne — Stranraer rail link	IRL/UK
Malpensa airport (Milan)	I
Fixed rail/road link between Denmark and Sweden (Øresund fixed link) including access routes	DK/S

———

Annex II

List of energy projects which the European Council has given priority status

France — Italy: electricity interconnection

Italy — Greece: electricity interconnection (cable)

Denmark: east-west electricity connection (cable)
        (not eligible for Structural Funds)

Portugal: natural gas network

Greece: natural gas network

Spain — Portugal: natural gas interconnections[1]

Spain — Portugal: electricity interconnections

Algeria — Morocco — European Union: gas pipeline

* * *

Russia — Belarus — Poland — European Union: gas pipeline[2]

---

[1] Including the introduction of natural gas in the Extremadura and Galicia regions of Spain.

[2] This project should also be shortlisted and studied although it has not yet reached the same stage as the other four gas schemes.

European Commission

Growth, competitiveness and employment
White Paper follow-up

Report on Europe and the global information society

Interim report on trans-European networks

Progress report on employment

Extracts of the conclusions of the Presidency of the Corfu European Council

Supplement 2/94 — Bull. EU

Luxembourg: Office for Official Publications of the European Communities

1994 — 134 pp. — 17.6 × 25.0 cm

ISBN 92-826-8547-0

Price (excluding VAT) in Luxembourg: ECU 7